**At Issue**

| Bilingual Education

# Other Books in the At Issue Series:

# At Issue

# | Bilingual Education

*Janel D. Ginn, Book Editor*

**GREENHAVEN PRESS**
*A part of Gale, Cengage Learning*

GALE
CENGAGE Learning·

Detroit • New York • San Francisco • New Haven, Conn • Waterville, Maine • London

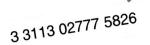

GALE
CENGAGE Learning

Christine Nasso, *Publisher*
Elizabeth Des Chenes, *Managing Editor*

© 2008 Greenhaven Press, a part of Gale, Cengage Learning.

*For more information, contact:*
Greenhaven Press
27500 Drake Rd.
Farmington Hills, MI 48331-3535
Or you can visit our Internet site at gale.cengage.com

Articles in Greenhaven Press anthologies are often edited for length to meet page require-ments. In addition, original titles of these works are changed to clearly present the main thesis and to explicitly indicate the author's opinion. Every effort is made to ensure that Greenhaven Press accurately reflects the original intent of the authors. Every effort has been made to trace the owners of copyrighted material.

ISBN-13: 978-0-7377-3912-1 (hardcover)
ISBN-13: 978-0-7377-3913-8 (pbk.)

Library of Congress Control Number: 2007938125

Printed in the United States of America
2 3 4 5 6 7 12 11 10 09 08

# Contents

# Introduction

When bilingual education was first introduced in the United States in 1968, Congress hoped to ensure that immigrants would receive a quality education even before they achieved proficiency in English. Bilingual education changed significantly over the ensuing decades, as research showed evidence that certain curricula worked better than others. New ideas such as dual language were introduced in schools, and some states banned bilingual education entirely. Today, many Americans have an opinion on bilingual education, and for most it is a matter of strong conviction.

Advocates of bilingual education explain that instructors in core subjects such as math, science, and social studies, should be provided in a child's native language so that an English as a Second Language (ESL) student can keep up with his or her grade level even before achieving English proficiency. This provides equal education to all. Stephen Krashen, professor emeritus of education at University of Southern California, wrote in 2005, "Developing literacy in the first language provides a shortcut to English literacy. Children learn to read much more easily in a language they understand, and once they can read in the primary language, they can rapidly transfer these reading skills into English. Teaching subject matter in the first language stimulates intellectual development and provides students with valuable knowledge that will help them understand instruction when it is presented in English."

In addition, proponents of dual-language programs, which place English and Spanish speakers together so students receive instruction in both languages, assert that this collaboration creates strong relationships between students because they must work together. At the same time, students achieve bilingual proficiency, which expands their career opportunities later in life.

Those who support English-only instruction point out that immersion is the best way to learn a new language, and that a delay in mastering English impedes a student's growth in all other academic subjects. In addition, they believe immigrants who cannot speak the native language of the country they live in are viewed as "outsiders," and will never assimilate. In a speech delivered to Congress on May 23, 2007, Roger Clegg, president and general counsel of the Center for Equal Opportunity, stated that learning English was one of the ten basic principles all Americans (native and immigrant) must adhere to:

"We simply have to be able to communicate with one another, and that means a common language, and that means English," Roger Clegg said. "So-called bilingual education, that is, teaching English to non-English speakers only slowly, in segregated classrooms, for only an hour or two a day has proved to be nonlingual: Students never learn English and their Spanish isn't so hot either."

It is interesting to note that in the debate about bilingual education, Spanish and English are the only two languages involved in the discussion. At a time when immigrants from hundreds of nations are arriving in the United States, and in an era where advocates for equal education are stronger and louder than ever before, why is no one demanding that schools offer classroom instruction in Chinese, Russian, French, or Arabic?

Perhaps it is because the bilingual education debate is not so much an issue of instruction, but of competing cultures. Spanish speakers are the largest minority in the United States, and in many states bordering Mexico, Hispanics comprise a higher percentage of the population than Caucasians. Many suggest there is strong resistance from Hispanics to assimilate into American ways of life. Insisting that their children receive an education in their native language is one more way Hispanic parents may maintain a separate culture.

Yet many times, it is Hispanic immigrants who oppose bilingual education with the most fervor. Parents resist school administration attempts to enroll their children in classrooms taught in Spanish. They maintain one of the reasons they came to America was so their children could learn English in the hopes it would give them better career opportunities than their Spanish-speaking parents are afforded.

If parents aren't the ones behind the bilingual education effort, who is? Many teachers and school administrators support the idea of teaching limited English proficiency (LEP) students in their native language so they do not fall behind in mathematics, science, or history while they are adapting to a new language. However, there are just as many professional educators who are opposed to using scarce funding to hire Spanish-speaking teachers who may actually be less proficient in English than their students.

Surprisingly, it is often politicians making the most noise about bilingual education. Political hopefuls make campaign promises to protect, reform, or eliminate bilingual education, while elected officials sign legislation for research, new instruction, and establishing official English in order to satisfy constituents and earn votes to further their political careers.

Amid the clamor surrounding the bilingual education issue coming from the local classroom as well as Capitol Hill, there is no clear answer to the question of which approach to teaching English proficiency in public schools works best. The authors in *At Issue: Bilingual Education* discuss the variety of opinions surrounding bilingual education in the following viewpoints.

# 1

# Education Must Respond to the Rising Immigrant Population

*Melissa Taylor Bell*

*Melissa Taylor Bell is the associate director of research at the Council of State Governments.*

*The American education system faces a huge challenge as immigrants continue entering the U.S. There is no consensus on the best way to teach non-English speakers and there is a growing shortage of teachers who are fluent in languages other than English. States are experimenting with new curricula, and federal funding helps with the financial burden of English education, but a practical solution is needed.*

As the level of immigration continues to rise, so does the number of children who need to be educated by the American educational system. According to a November 2003 article in the *New York Times*, American schools now educate approximately 11 million children of immigrants, including about 5.5 million who speak English poorly or not at all. Consequently, there are almost 5 million English language learners in grades K–12, which is almost a 100 percent increase over the past decade, according to The National Council of La Raza.

Language barriers pose certain challenges to state and local education officials. For one thing, there is no consensus on the best way to teach children with limited English skills. There are two major approaches to teaching this group of children. English as a Second Language [ESL] involves teaching children all subjects in modified English that they can understand more easily. The second approach, bilingual education, involves teaching children reading and writing skills in their native languages and then gradually shifting instruction to English. While ESL is more common than bilingual education, there is no consensus on which method is best or how long it takes for English language learners to become proficient in English.

## Different Approaches

Some states are also experimenting with ways to integrate curriculum content with language skills. Rather than providing ESL courses as a separate curriculum, for instance, some schools in Indiana have recognized the need to integrate content and language as an optimal way to educate ELL [English Language Learners] students.

*Some states are taking a comprehensive approach to educating ESL students by integrating early childhood education, adult literacy, or adult basic education, and parenting education.*

The state uses the Interdisciplinary Collaborative Program to help schools that display strong ESL needs link teachers who do not have ESL certification with content-area teachers. Professional development and peer collaboration fostered by the program assists the team of teachers in fusing language instruction with the content-area curriculum. The participating teachers attend two workshops per year and three classes at the Summer Language Minority Institute. Web-based conferencing and e-mail correspondence ensures ongoing support for teachers. The program is funded by a five-year $1 million grant from the U.S. Department of Education.

Some states are taking a comprehensive approach to educating ELL students by integrating early childhood education, adult literacy or adult basic education and parenting education. For this purpose, states have used Even Start—a federal program for improving the educational opportunities of low-income families. Designed to break the intergenerational cycle of poverty and illiteracy, the program has provided funding for 1,200 state-administered local projects.

For instance, Nebraska funds nine Even Start programs in metropolitan and rural areas through a competitive application process. All Nebraska Even Start programs have a large component that targets non-English-proficient families. Children up to age seven and a parent or adult caregiver who could benefit from intensive literacy services can participate in the program. A family remains enrolled in Even Start as long as one parent and one or more eligible children are participating and working toward meeting their literacy goals.

Wisconsin's Green Bay Even Start program brings together several agencies, including the Literacy Council, a regional community college and Compass Child Care to offer child care services while adults attend ESL classes. Later, children and their parents are united for a group activity.

## A Call to Action

While there is no consensus on teaching methods or how long to pursue these methods, states have learned that it costs more to educate non-English-speaking students than it does English speakers. Recent estimates from the Center for Special Education Finance suggest that expenditures on a child in an ESL or bilingual education program are 1.1 to 1.2 times the average expenditures on a student in a regular classroom.

In short, the number of immigrants and immigrants' children in American schools is on the rise. Because of education's importance in American society, educators and state policy-makers will continue to explore ways to teach immigrants and children of immigrants the skills they need to succeed socially and economically.

2

# Bilingual Education Is Detrimental to Everyone

*Peter Duignan*

*Peter Duignan is the author or editor of more than forty books, including* Making and Remaking America: Immigration into the United States. *He is also emeritus senior fellow and Lillick curator at the Hoover Institution at Stanford University.*

*The United States receives many immigrants each year, incorporating many world cultures into one nation; however, Hispanics resisted assimilation into American culture. By insisting on preferential treatment, especially in the area of bilingual education, immigrants place their children at a disadvantage and threaten the unity of the nation.*

Immigration has made and remade this country. Not only do immigrants not harm America but they have benefited it. The *Wall Street Journal* calls for high levels of immigration because it means more consumers, more workers, and a larger economy with new blood for the United States. Whereas Europe and Japan have aging populations and face shortages of tax money to care for their elderly, the United States, thanks to immigration, has a growing population. Immigrant labor, moreover, keeps prices, supplies, and services available and cheap.

In 1952, the McCarran-Walter Act allotted to each foreign country an annual quota for immigrants based on the proportion of people from that country present in America in 1920. This policy favored northern European immigrants but kept out southern and central Europeans. The next big change in immigration policy came in 1965, when President Lyndon Johnson abolished the national-origin quota system favoring Europe and adopted a system that favored the Western Hemisphere.

As immigration increased and the origins of immigrants changed, U.S. policies changed; the welfare state was enlarged and affirmative action and other programs benefited the new immigrants from Asia and the Western Hemisphere. Bilingualism and multiculturalism lessened the assimilation of the new immigrants in ways they had not influenced earlier arrivals from Europe.

## A Change in Immigration

Until the early decades of the twentieth century, immigrants were usually Europeans. Today most immigrants are from Asia, Mexico, Latin America, and the Caribbean. The newcomers have come more quickly and in greater numbers than previous waves of immigrants, especially through illegal entrance. They therefore have a bigger impact on population growth, the economy, schools, and the welfare system. They are harder to integrate than earlier immigrants were because there are fewer pressures on them to assimilate and learn English. Instead, bilingual education, multiculturalism, and ethnic clustering slow up the workings of the so-called melting pot.

Does this matter? America successfully absorbed Irish, Germans, Poles, and Jews, but things have changed. In the past we had a confident core culture. America insisted that newcomers assimilate and learn English—and they did. There was no bilingual education; there were no ethnic studies or affirmative action programs. The new immigrants are coming faster and in larger yearly numbers. These large numbers (one million a year plus 500,000 illegals) are proving harder to assimilate.

The new immigrants are arriving at a time when U.S. cultural self-reliance has eroded. Having learned from the civil rights struggle of black Americans, Mexican and Asian activists seek bilingual education and affirmative action for their own people while rejecting assimilation and Western culture. Latino activists demand ethnic studies programs in colleges and universities, group rights, and proportional representation in electoral districts, employment, the awarding of official contracts, and many other spheres of public life.

Latinos cluster in large neighborhoods to a greater extent than the foreigners who came here a century ago. Such clustering slows the learning of English and the rate of assimilation. Poor people who receive welfare benefits have fewer incentives to master English and adjust to the demands of American society. Latino immigrants, in particular, now make political demands of a kind not made by Sicilian or Greek immigrants a century ago. They are adopting the divisive and counterproductive stance of a racial minority. Their leaders demand privileges similar to those claimed for blacks.

In rejecting the melting pot concept, multiculturalists want to preserve immigrant culture and languages rather than absorb American culture. Those who oppose immigration hope to restrict the flow of immigrants so as to better assimilate the newcomers and promote the melting pot process. Otherwise, multiculturalism could lead to political fragmentation and then disaster. Restrictionists predict a stark picture of America as a Bosnia of continental proportions with a population of half a billion and dozens of contending ethnic groups, all lacking a sense of common nationhood, common culture, or political heritage.

## Bilingual Education—Helpful or Harmful?

In the past, the children of immigrants were educated in English only, which assimilated them in one generation. Nowadays, with bilingual education being imposed on millions of students—with large numbers of Spanish-speaking immigrants arriving each year—the assimilation process is longer and less successful. Indeed, today's children will take three generations to assimilate.

Education has been a contentious subject since the Civil Rights Act (1964) and the Bilingual Education Act (1968) decreed that children should be instructed in their native tongues for a transitional year while they learned English but were to transfer to all-English classrooms as soon as possible. These prescriptions were ignored by bilingual enthusiasts. English was neglected, and Spanish-language instruction and cultural maintenance became the norm.

Bilingual education was said to be essential, allowing Hispanics to gain a new sense of pride and resist Americanization. The *Lau v. Nichols* (1974) case stands out as a landmark: after the decision, bilingual education moved away from a transitional year to a multiyear plan to teach the children of immigrants in their home language before teaching them in English. This facilitation theory imprisoned Spanish speakers in classrooms where essentially only Spanish was taught; bilingual education became Spanish cultural maintenance, with English limited to 30 minutes a day. As a result, Spanish speakers were literate in neither Spanish nor English.

---

*English plays a crucial role in cultural assimilation, a proposition evident also to minority people who argue that Spanish-language instruction in the public schools will leave their children badly disadvantaged when they graduate.*

---

Linda Chavez, president of the Center for Equal Opportunity, accuses these advocates of bilingual education of being politicized and manipulated by cultural activists. The programs they favor have failed, she claims, and have undermined the future of the Latino children they were meant to help. Her criticisms are supported by the evidence. Latinos taught in bilingual programs test behind peers taught in English-only classrooms, drop out of school at a high rate, and are trapped in low-skilled, low-paying jobs.

As noted earlier, the problem began in 1974 when the Supreme Court ignored 200 years of English-only instruction in American schools and said that students who did not speak English must receive special treatment from local schools. *Lau v. Nichols* allowed an enormous expansion of bilingual education. For example, in 1968, the U.S. Office for Civil Rights began a small program to educate Mexican-American children; by 1996, it had expanded to an $8 billion a year industry.

As the program grew, the initial objective to teach English to Spanish speakers for one or two years was perverted into an effort to Hispanicize, not Americanize, Spanish speakers. The federal program insists that 75 percent of education tax dollars be spent on bilingual education—that is, long-term native-language programs, not English as a second language. Asians, Africans, and Europeans are all in mainstream classes and receive extra training in English-as-a-second-language programs for a few hours a day. Hispanic students, in contrast, are taught in Spanish 70 to 80 percent of the time.

---

*If the number [of] immigrants is reduced, bilingualism eliminated, and Americanization encouraged, there will be little danger to U.S. unity.*

---

The old total immersion system still works best; the longer students stay in segregated bilingual programs, the less successful they are in school. Even after 28 years of bilingual programs, the dropout rate for Latinos is the highest in the country. In Los Angeles, the Latino students dropped out at double the state average (44 percent over four years of high school). Special English-language instruction from day one gets better results than Spanish-language instruction for most of the day.

A higher degree of proficiency in English should be required by applicants for naturalization in the United States. A citizen should be able to read all electoral literature in English—no more foreign-language ballots. Educators in publicly funded high schools who believe that their task is to maintain the immigrant cultural heritage should be opposed. Such endeavors are best left to parents, churches, Saturday schools, and the extended family.

The role of the public-school teacher is to instruct students in English and American culture and political values. English plays a crucial role in cultural assimilation, a proposition evident also to minority people who argue that Spanish-language instruction in the public schools will leave their children badly disadvantaged when they graduate.

There is, however, hope in the battle against bilingual education. In 1998 California passed Proposition 227, calling for an end to bilingual education. If bilingual education is limited to one or two years for non-English-speaking children, who are then taught only in English, the U.S. school system will be able to assimilate students to English as it did before 1965. . . .

## What About the Future?

What kind of a United States do Americans want for the future? Most Americans feel somewhat ambivalent about immigration—their own forebears may, after all, have come from abroad—even as they tell pollsters they want immigration reduced. Americans are particularly opposed to illegal immigration, although not to undocumented aliens as individuals.

Statisticians in the Census Bureau forecast that by 2050, Caucasians will barely form a majority, with Hispanics far exceeding black Americans as the largest minority. But these forecasts may be called into question. For instance, such predictions take little or no account of lower birthrates for immigrants or intermarriage with other social groups. The intermarriage rate is high both for Latino and Asian people in the United States; the rate, moreover, increases from one generation to the next.

The United States will certainly be more ethnically and racially mixed in the future. It is not sure, however, how this amalgam will be composed, especially as future immigration patterns may change in an unexpected manner. If the number [of] immigrants is reduced, bilingualism eliminated, and Americanization encouraged, there will be little danger to U.S. unity.

# 3

# English-Only Requirements Are Anti-Immigration

*Rebecca L. Weber*

*Rebecca L. Weber is a writer for NEA Today.*

*Around half of all states currently have statutes or constitutional amendments in place declaring English the official language in the workplace and in schools. While encouraging immigrants to assimilate into American culture is important, laws punishing students for not speaking English in school send a message that foreigners are not welcome in the United States and fail to help ESL students succeed in the classroom.*

Zachariah Rubio unintentionally made national news [in 2005] when a peer asked him—in Spanish—to borrow a dollar. "No hay problema," he replied, a quip that got him suspended from his Kansas City, Kansas, high school. Although the superintendent soon revoked the punishment, the incident reflects the changing nature of bilingual education.

About half of all states now have some form of English-only statute or constitutional amendment in place—at a time when more people than ever before live in homes where English is not spoken. Some 14 million of them are children, and in a growing number of places, lawmakers are changing the way they learn English.

In California and Massachusetts, students have just a year to get up to speed before completing the rest of their course-

Rebecca L. Weber, "Something to Talk About: English-Only Laws Are Restricting More Than Just What's Being Said," *NEA Today*, vol. 25, November 2006, p. 25. Copyright 2006 National Education Association of the United States. Reproduced by permission.

work in English. Arizona—where one in four residents is His-panic—has the strongest English-only education laws, all but barring teachers from using non-English words.

Bilingual educators in these states find themselves having to follow the letter of such laws. "It is anti-immigration," says Tempe, Arizona, elementary school teacher Nidia Lias of the policies that prohibit her from speaking Spanish to her stu-dents. Her colleague, Molly Cota, had to remove all the Spanish-language materials from her classroom. Teaching aides now translate only on a limited basis, and simple clarifications are mostly a thing of the past. Mentioning the dyeing of eggs led to confusion for one of Cota's first-graders, who asked, "¿Como se puede morir los huevos?" (How can the eggs die?)

## A Disconnect Between Rules and Education

Some English-language learners (ELLs) have also been shifted out of specialized classrooms. Cota now has half a dozen in a class of 22; the rest are divided equally among other teach-ers—some of whom, she says, have not been trained ad-equately in bilingual methods such as total body response and emphasis on visuals. "A weekend class is not going to do it," says Lias, who compensates in her sixth-grade classroom by using color-coded number lines posted on the walls, constant repetition, and pointing. "I spent years working on my ELL, and my colleagues did, too."

When it comes to learning a language, kids are like sponges. Immerse them in English, and they'll be fluent in no time—or so goes the conventional wisdom.

---

*While just 8 percent of the country's teenagers have im-migrated to the United States, almost one in four teen dropouts is foreign-born.*

---

English-only advocates say that assimilation and mastering English are crucial to success in school, the workforce, and society. But children who can speak English on the playground can't necessarily comprehend grade-level academic content in English. Research suggests that kids will eventually become more proficient in both English and their mother tongue if they first become literate in their home language. A report sponsored by the National Literacy Panel for Language Minority Children, for instance, found that students with native language instruction fare better than English immersion students do.

English-only laws are also making it more difficult to attract bilingual education students to the profession, in part because they're leery of environments where speaking another language is considered a liability, says Jill Kerper Mora, an NEA member who teaches education at San Diego State University.

## Nobody's Winning

The laws are also causing confusion. In Massachusetts, local—and changing—interpretations of sheltered English immersion (SEI) have caused schools to shift between mainstreaming and pulling out ELLs. Educators have, at different times, been offered work as lower-paid tutors, shuffled between buildings, or laid off.

Still, ELL teachers acknowledge the surface appeal of English-only laws. "Even somebody who has been teaching for a while [who's] not exposed to second language learners, and hasn't been educated in the process of learning a second language, [wouldn't understand that] it takes years to achieve an academic language," says Leah Palmer, an SEI teacher in Brockton, Massachusetts.

Given high-stakes testing and other pressures, that gradual learning curve can take a toll. While just 8 percent of the country's teenagers have immigrated to the United States, almost one in four teen dropouts is foreign-born. "Right now, the message is, we don't want you here, but we expect you to assimilate," says Mora. "Well, which is it?"

# 4

# Learning Native Languages First Helps Students Learn English

*Jill Wu*

*Jill Wu is a graduate student in the Applied Linguistics Program at the University of Colorado in Denver.*

*When it comes to teaching English language learners, no one method is guaranteed to help all children succeed in language acquisition. However, research supports that students who are proficient at reading and writing in their native language first are far more likely to succeed at learning English.*

As the number of English language learners in U.S. schools increases, experts continue to seek ways to effectively educate these students. Those who argue for English immersion and for other practices emphasizing English-only instruction believe that this approach avoids segregating language learners, promotes assimilation of immigrants, and helps students learn English as quickly as possible. Bilingual education, they feel, divides society and limits Latinos' opportunities. These supporters cite evidence of ineffective bilingual programs and stories of immigrant children who have succeeded in immersion programs.

Many second-language acquisition experts and others counter that immersion programs have not been proven effective. They believe that bilingual education programs, which provide initial instruction in students' first language, are more successful in helping students acquire English. For example, [James] Crawford [reported in a 1998 article] that students in programs that stressed native language instruction had much larger increases in English reading and math skills than did students in English immersion programs or programs that stressed early transition to English.

My experiences teaching English language learners in three different settings help to explain why bilingual education programs sometimes work and sometimes do not. These experiences demonstrate what advocates on both sides of the issue often fail to realize: that not all bilingual programs are the same; that no program will guarantee success for all students in all settings; and that English language learners often receive confusing and inconsistent instruction whether their program is called bilingual or immersion.

---

*[S]tudies have shown that English language learners in dual immersion programs have higher academic achievement than do those taught in English immersion programs.*

---

## A Dual Language Classroom

My first experience with bilingual education was in a dual language immersion school in Wisconsin. In this setting, native English speakers and native Spanish speakers learned together in the same classroom. Instruction began in Spanish for both English and Spanish speakers. As students acquired a good reading base in Spanish, we gradually incorporated English. By 5th grade, students received half of their instruction in each language.

Unlike transitional bilingual education, which views native language instruction as a means to learn English, dual language programs aim to produce students who are fluent in both languages. According to speech-language experts [Celeste] Roseberry-McKibbin and [Alejandro] Brice, studies have shown that English language learners in dual immersion programs have higher academic achievement than do those taught in English immersion programs. By taking an enrichment approach rather than a remedial approach, dual language immersion produces bilingual and biliterate students who can switch effortlessly from one language to the other.

As I worked in this school, I realized why the dual language immersion approach was successful. No one group had the dominant language—the language of power. The native Spanish speakers felt empowered, not only because they acquired literacy and found success in their own language, but also because they were models for the English-speaking students. The English-speaking students also benefited by acquiring a second language at an early age.

In 1st grade, these students were exciting to teach. They spurred one another on. Classroom discourse naturally alternated between English and Spanish, unlike the conversation in many bilingual classrooms where students never speak English except when talking to the teacher.

Socially, this approach had powerful implications. At the beginning of the year, I saw many shy Spanish speakers who congregated together. As I taught these students to read in Spanish, they became more confident in their Spanish literacy skills, but they were still reluctant to use English. Slowly, however, the native Spanish speakers and the native English speakers began to communicate with one another. As students interacted, they learned English and Spanish in meaningful ways, communicating with their peers on the playground and in the classroom. When one of the English speakers had a birthday party at her house, I had the opportunity to see the children interact outside the classroom. I was surprised when Leah, a native Spanish speaker whom I had never heard use

English, spoke in fluent English as she communicated with her English-speaking friends at the party.

## Bilingual Education Inconsistently Applied

When I left Wisconsin, I was enthusiastic about dual immersion bilingual education and all that it could accomplish. My next school district, in Colorado, had recently adopted a transitional bilingual model in which Spanish-speaking students would acquire literacy in their primary language and then gradually achieve literacy in English.

I took a job as a 1st grade bilingual teacher. Most of my students were Spanish speakers who did not know any English. I was surprised to discover that they had no letter-recognition skills—in fact, no literacy skills at all. I soon figured out that the problem stemmed from their kindergarten experience the year before.

The district-adopted transitional bilingual policy had not yet filtered down from the central office to the school level, so my 1st grade students had not received reading readiness instruction in their primary language. Instead, the school had placed all of the native Spanish speakers in one kindergarten class with an English-speaking teacher who made little effort to make English comprehensible to them. These students spoke Spanish in almost all settings of their lives. But for a few hours each day, they came to school and listened to a lady speak English. The input they received was similar to what we might hear from Charlie Brown's teacher—"wa, wa, wa, wa." Although some of my students had learned their colors and how to say words like bathroom, they had no phonemic awareness or letter-recognition skills in either language.

When I tested the students' knowledge of letter-sound correlation, I got another shock. I asked students which words started with the A sound and gave them some examples of Spanish words from alphabet posters with corresponding pictures. The students insisted that manzana started with an A sound, abeja started with a B sound, helado started with an I sound, and so on. I was confused. Why couldn't the students hear the beginning sounds of these words?

Then I realized what had happened. Manzana means apple in English; abeja means bee; and helado means ice cream. In kindergarten, the students had memorized the pictures that go with the letters in the English alphabet. They had never learned how to say apple, bee, or ice cream in English; they had translated the words into Spanish. They had never learned to hear the sounds; they had merely learned that the picture of a manzana somehow matches the symbol A.

Although the students' kindergarten instruction had given them almost no prereading skills, I was eager to teach them to read in Spanish, as directed by the district's new bilingual policy. We spent hours every day working on letter sounds. Simultaneously, I taught other core subjects (math, social studies, and science) in Spanish, gradually incorporating more English and developing the students' oral English skills as we discussed concepts from these subjects.

## Encouraging Signs of Progress

As the students and I struggled through the first four months, I began to wonder when they would make progress learning to read in any language. Many of them still struggled with blending letters. Eventually, however, it all seemed to click. A few students started to read, and the rest soon followed.

Because Spanish is a completely phonetic language, when students know how to decipher syllables they can decode almost anything. Learning how to read in Spanish empowered my students. After their Spanish literacy skills became more solid and their oral English skills improved, many of them began to read in English. This time, the goal seemed easily attainable because all their reading skills from Spanish transferred to English. This experience confirmed the views of language experts who have found that once we can read in one language, we do not need to learn how to read all over again. In addition, my students had the English vocabulary to comprehend what they read; they were delighted when they could sound out C-O-W and know what the word meant.

Although this method of teaching was not quite as natural or easy as teaching in the dual language school in Wisconsin, it still worked and gave me many reasons to support transitional bilingual education. If I had taught the students to read in English initially, it would have taken much longer for them to acquire literacy. Because I taught core subjects in Spanish, students could keep up with grade-level content because they could understand what they were learning. Their success learning in one language motivated them to succeed in the second.

---

*A class that could have helped student's transition into reading in English became the class to dump all the students with "needs."*

---

Another 1st grade class of English language learners in the school that year had a different experience. After their bilingual teacher left early in the year, they received instruction from a full-time substitute who spoke no Spanish. When my students went on to 2nd grade, their teachers told me that they were much better prepared and spoke and wrote better English than the students who had been taught in an English-only class. My students had acquired English in a natural way, and they had transferred their Spanish reading skills smoothly to English.

## Incoherent Programs

Later, I moved to 4th grade at a different school in the same district. I was excited by the change; I wanted to see firsthand how older students were gaining English literacy skills.

To meet the needs of the bilingual students, the school had decided to group the 4th and 5th grade English language learners for reading. Two teachers would teach a group of 4th and 5th graders who were performing on or near grade level, which included many native Spanish speakers who had transitioned to English. Another teacher would teach a group of Spanish-speaking students who had just moved to the United States and were not ready to transition. I would teach the group of students who were just beginning to transition to English literacy. I was excited about teaching these students, assuming that like my 1st graders, they would just need a little push to master learning and reading in English.

Unfortunately, the reality soon became clear. All the students in my reading group were performing far below grade level and lacked many reading skills. They did not have the same motivation that the 1st graders had displayed. How had the bilingual program failed them? Why, by the time they reached 4th grade, were these 30 kids still reading at the 1st grade level or below?

## Ineffective Grouping

At first, I thought that the practice of grouping our students by language level for reading instruction sounded wonderful; the students' needs would be similar and I would be able to teach them more effectively. Unfortunately, my group included not just the bilingual students, but all students who came into 4th or 5th grade reading at the 1st grade level or below. This meant that the class contained struggling English readers who spoke Spanish, the school's few Vietnamese and Cambodian students, and many of the special education and emotionally disturbed students.

A class that could have helped student's transition into reading in English became the class to dump all the students with "needs." But just because these students struggled to read did not mean that they struggled to read for the same reasons. Effective instruction for the class's English language learners would not necessarily address the needs of other struggling students with different needs.

---

*Instead of creating bilingual students, we had created students who could speak two languages to some degree but who could not read or comprehend academic material in either.*

---

Even the English language learners in the group had experienced many different instructional environments. Some had attended the same school since kindergarten and had received Spanish language reading instruction through 1st grade, with a transition to English in 2nd grade. Others were new immigrants to the United States. Some had recently moved from other districts or from other schools in the same district that were unable to staff bilingual classes. Because of high mobility rates, some students had switched several times between Spanish language and English language instruction.

## Reading Skills and Background Knowledge

Reading involves many complex processes, and learning to read presents extra challenges for second-language learners. [A study released in 2001 by the Center for Applied Linguistics in Washington, DC] discovered that English language learners acquire decoding skills easily, but they struggle more than native English speakers in their reading comprehension. By the time these students read to the end of a sentence or a book, they may have no idea what either means. They have a hard time monitoring their comprehension.

My 4th and 5th graders' struggles confirmed [these] observations. My students' biggest challenge was their lack of background knowledge and vocabulary. They had no frame of reference to understand the books we studied. I often heard such questions as "What is the ocean?", "What is a zoo?", and "Do we really have mountains near here?" Because many of the students had never left their neighborhoods, a book about life under the sea posed difficulties for them. They not only had to work on their decoding, fluency, and vocabulary, but they also had to comprehend content that was outside their realm of experience.

Second-language acquisition experts say that developing students' first language gives them subject-matter knowledge that enables them to comprehend what they read and hear in English. I found that many of my students had not been given the opportunity to develop skills in any language. Perhaps the students had been transitioned too quickly, before they developed solid reading skills and background knowledge in Spanish, and thus they did not have fully formed skills to transfer over to English. Consequently, they had not experienced success that would motivate them. Instead of creating bilingual students, we had created students who could speak two languages to some degree but who could not read or comprehend academic material in either.

*My experience suggests that students acquire a second language most easily when they develop literacy skills and content knowledge in their native language, have opportunities to interact with English-speaking peers, and learn with students of different ability levels.*

## Success in Spite of Frustration

In spite of the barriers that the system had put in their way, many of my students learned and progressed. Hard work and belief in students can accomplish a lot. And a few students far exceeded expectations. What accounted for their success?

Maria and Marcos, two 5th graders in my reading class, had only been in the United States a little more than a year, but they were ready to transition to reading in English. Both progressed to near grade-level proficiency in one year, surpassing other students who had been in the country longer.

One of the reasons Maria and Marcos succeeded was that they had a solid education in their native language. They were fluent readers in Spanish and had strong background knowledge. Researchers have found that the amount of formal schooling a student receives in the first language is the strongest predictor of how that student will perform academically in the second and that the most successful English language learners are those who have maintained bilingualism and a strong connection with their family's culture. Marcos and Maria could connect whatever they read about in English with knowledge and concepts that they had learned in Spanish. Thus, they felt successful and motivated.

## Experience Supports Research

For English language learners, becoming fluent in English is a challenging process that cannot be accomplished in a single year. Because of accountability pressures, the debate that surrounds bilingual education, and the panic to get students on grade level, schools often push students rapidly into English-only instruction, where they flounder or get labeled as needing special education.

My experience suggests that students acquire a second language most easily when they develop literacy skills and content knowledge in their native language, have opportunities to interact with English-speaking peers, and learn with students of different ability levels. We need to remember that the fastest way is not necessarily the most effective way. When advocates push for English fluency at any cost, they fail to realize that the cost may be students' literacy and academic development.

# 5

# English Should Not Replace a Child's Native Language

*Mariana Souto-Manning*

*Mariana Souto-Manning, a Latina immigrant from Brazil, is an elementary school teacher in the state of Georgia.*

*Contrary to the long-standing belief in the American education community, the human brain is not limited to learning only one language. In fact, research shows that the more languages a person learns, the stronger their mental stamina. Teachers and parents of ESL students must encourage children to retain the ability to speak their native language in addition to achieving fluency in English.*

In recent years, the population of the United States has been experiencing significant demographic, linguistic, and cultural changes. In the Southeast, in cities and towns where 10 years ago English was the language that would almost exclusively be heard in grocery stores and on radios, Spanish has become common. Immigration has peaked in states such as Georgia, with 300% Latino growth over the last 10 years. Ninety percent of newcomers to the United States have come from Latin American, Asian and African countries. With the surge of immigration, more and more bilingual children will enter schools. Today, one in five children in the United States lives in an immigrant family.

As an elementary school teacher in a school district with urban characteristics in the Southeastern United States, I often

Mariana Souto-Manning, "A Critical Look at Bilingualism Discourse in Public Schools: Autoethnographic Reflections of a Vulnerable Observer," *Bilingual Research Journal*, vol. 30, no. 2, Summer 2006, pp. 559–577. Copyright 2006 © National Association for Bilingual Education. All rights reserved. Reproduced by permission.

wondered why so many second-generation immigrants did not retain their heritage languages. Many of my students whose parents immigrated from Mexico and other Latin American countries spoke very little Spanish. As a proponent of bilingualism, I often encouraged them to speak their heritage language at home. . . .

## From Theory to Reality

I didn't realize how hard it was to raise a child bilingually until I became a mother myself and started the challenging task of raising my own child bilingually. I realized the [1922] misconception [by O. Jespersen] that the "brain effort required to master the two languages instead of one certainly diminishes the child's power of learning other things which might and ought to be learnt" is still widespread in schools today in many teachers' discursive repertoires. According to this view, a child's intellectual capacity is limited, due to the conception that bilinguals think less efficiently because the brain stores two linguistic systems. From such a stance, learning two or more languages might be deemed detrimental to children and adults alike.

I was not fully aware of the prejudices towards Latinos until I gave birth to my son. As soon as he was born, still under the effects of medication to alleviate the partum pains, I was approached by a hospital worker seeking information about my newborn. She asked his name, my name and his father's name. She went on to ask his race. I looked at my blue-eyed son; he appeared White to me. I replied White, believing it was one of the possibilities. She immediately looked at me, a Latina immigrant, and said that he could not be "pure White," after all, I was not White. I guess my brownness had polluted the white color of his father. "What are the other options?" I asked. She said, "African American, Pacific Islander, and Other." I had no choice but to define my son as "Other."

Since then, I realized how the institutional discourse was already serving to otherize an infant.

Thinking that it was merely an issue of institutional discourse, I tried to get past that very uncomfortable moment, as a nurse pushed me in my wheelchair from the birthing room to the maternity room where I would spend my next 48 hours. As I arrived there, I could not help but write about the painful incident I had experienced, in hopes of removing it from my body. I wrote and wrote as my husband and mother watched the first baby bath and left me alone in the room. When my son finally returned to the room, I felt as if I could forget that experience and hoped that it had been an isolated case. I looked at his angelic face, and questioned whether anyone would have the courage to be prejudiced against such a lovable being.

*ELLs have historically been overreferred to special education due to inappropriate assessments and assignment to lower-performing instructional settings.*

Friends came to visit and shared with me some of their parenting tips. As I was a teacher in a local elementary school, many teacher colleagues came to visit, most of whom were English speaking. My mother, who had come from Brazil and is conversant in Portuguese, Spanish, and French, sat in the room without understanding much, smiling at the amusement of my friends, and at their coos as they tried to communicate with a newborn child. Many asked questions, but one particular interaction remained in my mind for much too long. Joyce (pseudonym), a friend of mine who taught special education at a local school, asked after hearing me answer my mother's questions in Portuguese, "You are not going to speak Portuguese to him, are you?" In framing the question in such a biased way, Joyce had hoped that I would avoid conflict . . . and agree with her. My unexpected answer that I would speak Portuguese to him prompted a very quick answer drawing on her expert knowledge. Joyce lowered her voice, as she said, "You know, if you speak Portuguese to him, he'll end up in special ed." Joyce's advice was aimed at aiding me, not hurting or confronting me. I could not go any further at that point, so I smiled. As my face smiled, my heart cried. It cried for my son, and for all other children who spoke languages other than English.

Joyce, a White, middle-class, monolingual, middle-aged, very talented and well-intentioned teacher holding a master's degree in education, had over 15 years of experience teaching special education classes at the elementary school level in high-poverty urban and rural areas in the Southeast. She had echoed the institutional discourse on bilingualism. Early [1977] studies of the academic, intellectual, and social achievements of bilingual children generally showed that they were [according to W. E. Lambert] "behind in school, retarded in measured intelligence and socially adrift" when compared to monolingual children. Joyce was agreeing with an understanding of bilingualism which was dismantled by research long ago but still has a strong hold on practitioners' minds in schools today.

## The Truth Behind the Research

To develop a better understanding of how bilingualism was defined in school settings, and the discourses shaping the educational experiences of bilingual children in elementary schools in the Southeast, I collected my own journal entries and interviewed Joyce, a teacher who taught in another public school. I kept a reflective journal in which I documented my experiences as a bilingual mother and immigrant teacher and took detailed fieldnotes of incidents happening at the school where I taught. . . .

For more than 30 years solid empirical evidence has shown the positive relationship between bilingual ability and intellectual functioning. Although the evidence indicates definite cognitive advantages for bilingual children, the stereotype of negative consequences persists. Professionals in the area of education propagate these institutional discourses, as many regard bilingualism as a deficit in their philosophical beliefs and sponsor this idea by incorporating it in their narratives and advice giving, including my friend Joyce. According to [L.] Tse (2001), research in the area of language acquisition and development actually points to bilingualism as a resource, rather than a deficit: "Not only do we appear to have infinite capacity for language learning, but knowing one language may help a learner pick up a second better and faster because it means not having to start from scratch."

---

*In the United States, bilingualism is still reticently associated with minority populations. Worldwide, however, bilingualism is the norm, rather than the exception, as over half of the people in the world are bilingual.*

---

A recent study [by S. L. Deno] reported that a "problem confronting schools in the United States is the dramatically increasing proportion of students whose first language is not English," casting English language learners (ELLs) in terms of a problem. Despite seeing ELLs as problems, this same study recognized the inadequacy of current achievement tests in assessing ELLs. According to Deno:

Many achievement tests draw heavily on background knowledge of the American culture in structuring questions. Among other problems that exist because of the lack of technically adequate procedures is how to distinguish ELL students who are having difficulty learning because of their lack of proficiency in English from ELL students whose struggles also stem from special disabilities.

ELLs have historically been overreferred to special education due to inappropriate assessments and assignment to lower-performing instructional settings. . . .

## Special Education Is Not a Solution

Multiple studies over the last two decades have pointed towards the likelihood that once a student is referred to special education, he or she will qualify to receive such services and be identified with a label. Referrals are significantly influenced by teacher beliefs and attitudes towards a student. Teacher beliefs are partly based on content-area performance. ELLs tend to perform significantly lower than non-ELL White students in reading, writing, math and science due to lack of equity in achievement tests. . . .

## Hoping for a Better Tomorrow

Research proposes that the acquisition and development of two languages augments one's language processing and that different processing systems develop to serve two linguistic systems. Nevertheless, the perception of children's brains as buckets preprogrammed for the development of a single language is still commonly employed and espoused. Temporary delays in the development of expressive English language in early bilingual development have served as examples of how bilingualism hinders long-term cognitive development. This could not be further from the truth. . . . Instead of thinking of bilingualism as a malady that affects part of the population, against which teachers need to fight, we, educators and parents, need to start promoting bilingualism as augmenting and sophisticating children's thought processes, and serving as a resource for all children.

In the United States, bilingualism is still reticently associated with minority populations. Worldwide, however, bilingualism is the norm, rather than the exception, as over half of the people in the world are bilingual. If bilingual children are not to be left behind, or stacked sideways in special education classrooms, so that their test scores will not count against adequate yearly progress mandated by the No Child Left Behind Act (2002), parents, educators, and interested parties, must continue promoting bilingualism as a resource in schools.

# 6

# English Instruction Could Lead to Heritage Language Resistance

*Alejandra Rodriguez-Galindo and Jo Worthy*

*Alejandra Rodriguez-Galindo and Jo Worthy conducted this study for the University of Texas at Austin.*

*Latino immigrant parents who do not learn to speak English encourage their children to take their bilingual education seriously. These parents hope that by speaking Spanish at home and English in school, their children will be able to achieve a better life. For some children, the stress of learning two languages and the pressure to serve as their parents' translators causes them to resist learning Spanish. This leads to communication breakdown in families and frustration among parents who fear their children will lose their heritage language.*

Taking steps to learn the language of their adopted country is often the first course of action that many immigrants take upon their arrival. Reasons for wanting to be conversant in the language of the new country include simply surviving and getting around, gaining employment, sharing a sense of identity with other citizens, personal enrichment, and, in the case of parents, helping their children negotiate school matters. Unfortunately, many immigrants to the United States, especially those who live in poverty, often find intractable barri-

Alejandra Rodriguez-Galindo and Jo Worthy, "*Mi Hija Vale Dos Personas*: Latino Immigrant Parents' Perspectives About Their Children's Bilingualism," *Bilingual Research Journal*, vol. 30, no. 2, Summer 2006, pp. 579–601. Copyright 2006 © National Association for Bilingual Education. All rights reserved. Reproduced by permission.

ers to learning English. Despite valiant efforts, the vast majority do not learn enough to communicate functionally or secure jobs that promise anything beyond simple survival. Ironically, many immigrants are treated with scorn because they are perceived as taking jobs from citizens and as not wanting to fit in by learning English. . . .

The initial rationale behind bilingual education was that transfer of knowledge and expertise to a new language is best accomplished when the learner is cognitively proficient in the first language. In practice, this should mean that students develop academic proficiency in their first language before being expected to study cognitively demanding concepts and materials in their second language. However, bilingual education programs since the late 1970s have become more transitional in nature. Concurrently, the academic proficiency criterion line has been blurred to the extent that many children are moved to full English instruction prematurely. . . .

It should come as no surprise, then, that despite the label "bilingual," few programs provide instruction designed to help students communicate, read, or write beyond basic proficiency in their native languages. Most bilingual programs in the United States are, in effect, remedial or compensatory programs, as the primary objective is for students to "graduate" to English instruction. Students' first language is seen as a vehicle for promoting English learning. As soon as this goal is realized, the first language has outlived its usefulness in the minds of many educators.

The loudest voices heard in discussions about bilingualism and bilingual education are typically those with a high degree of social and cultural capital—researchers, policymakers, and educators. We were interested in learning from immigrant parents with few social and economic resources about their perspectives on their children's bilingualism. We also considered it important to learn from those who have a personal stake in the hotly contested issue of bilingual education. The parents were interviewed during a study about the language use of their children, who were fifth graders in a bilingual education program in an urban elementary school in the Southwest. In that study, we concluded that, although the students had been schooled in a relatively nurturing bilingual environment, they were beginning to experience societal pressures to assimilate and were aware that these pressures would greatly increase in the future. . . .

---

*English proficiency was considered essential [by parents] for doing well in school, getting a good job, fitting into U.S. society, and leading a satisfying, successful life.*

---

## Parents' Perspective on Language

Although parents were grateful for their own ability to survive without knowing English, they wanted more for their children than to simply get by. They wanted them to thrive, and for this English was seen as a necessity. English proficiency was considered essential for doing well in school, getting a good job, fitting into U.S. society, and leading a satisfying, successful life. Isabel's mother shared that her older daughter, Elena, who was 13 when the family arrived in the United States, never learned English well enough to pass her classes and eventually dropped out of school. The mother had also observed Elena's struggles to find a job and had concluded that English was an important commodity in the workplace:

*Porque puede conseguir un trabajo mejor. Y si una persona va a una tienda y no habla español y no hay nadie que hable el inglés, pues se va a ir el cliente. Y aun así pues, si tienen alguien que hable inglés, se queda el cliente. Es mejor para un trabajo para ella [habla dos idiomas]. Cualquiera.* (Because you can get a better job. And if a person goes to a store and doesn't speak Spanish and there's no one there who speaks English, then the client will leave. And if you have someone who speaks English, the client will stay. It's better for a job for her [to speak two languages]. Any job.)

Parents also mentioned that they wanted their children to learn English so they could help younger siblings, who were receiving English instruction at a younger age. It was becoming increasingly difficult for parents to help the younger children with their homework or read to them, and they counted on the older children to help bridge this gap. All were adamant, then, in their desires for their children to learn English well. As Sofía's mother said, "*Les digo yo, pues, 'Echele ganas.' Lo que yo quiero es que aprendan el inglés.*" (I tell them, 'Try hard.' What I want is for them to learn English.)

---

*Perhaps due to the elevated status of English, negative messages about speaking Spanish, students' desires to assimilate, and efforts by the school and parents, developing English proficiency was not a major struggle for most of these students.*

---

*Being bilingual: "Para mí es importante los dos, el español y el inglés."*

Parents also wanted their children to continue speaking Spanish, with the most common reason being communication with their own families and maintaining the customs and culture of their home countries. Yolanda's mother explained: "*Si yo la hubiera dejado a puro inglés, no me podría comunicar yo con ella.*" (If I were to allow only English, I couldn't communicate with her.) David's mother remarked that she was happy to see that he was speaking Spanish as well as English at school. This was David's first year in the school and his first year in a bilingual class; he had been in ESL classes, where Spanish was not spoken, through fourth grade: "*Pues, yo creo que está bien [ser bilingüe] porque pues él tiene que mantenerlo [el español]. Como quien dice, 'educado aquí, pero es de México.' O sea, el tiene que mantener, como quien dice, dos culturas.*"

(Well, I believe [being bilingual] is good because he has to maintain [Spanish]. As they say, 'Educated here, but he is from Mexico.' That is, he has to maintain, as they say, two cultures.) . . .

Parents agreed that being bilingual was the apex of language learning. As Julio's mother said, "*Se dice, 'Se desenvuelve la persona que habla dos idiomas.'*" (They say, 'A person who speaks two languages shows more confidence.') Not only would bilingualism help them maintain their linguistic and cultural roots but, as Maricela's father said:

> "*La persona vale más cuando está más preparada. Entonces no quisiera que perdiera su español. Al contrario, que lo perfeccione más, al iqual que el inglés. Y pudiera hablar otro idioma [además del inglés y el español], pues sería mucho mejor.*" (A better-prepared person is worth more. So I wouldn't want her to lose her Spanish. On the contrary, she should perfect it more, the same as English. And if she could speak another language [in addition to English and Spanish], well, that would be even better.)

Every parent had heard or seen firsthand that jobs and pay were better for bilinguals. For example, Andrés' mother found her job opportunities limited by her inability to speak English. In contrast, Andrés' older sister was fluent in both languages. She worked as an interpreter and, despite being an undocumented resident, rarely lacked employment. And for those who were born in the United States (and thus, were automatically citizens), the opportunities were thought to be even greater, as Diana's father explained: "*Porque creemos, y se ha comprobado, que los que son bilingües tienen un poquito más de oportunidades, y los que son bilingües ganan un poquito más.*" (Because we believe, and it has been proven, that bilinguals have somewhat better job opportunities and earn a little more.) . . .

## Evidence of Spanish Erosion

Most parents saw evidence that their children were gradually becoming proficient users of English, as virtually all young immigrants do. A worry among many parents was the opposite problem—erosion of Spanish. Even though all parents spoke only Spanish to their children, more than half expressed concern that their children were forgetting or becoming less fluent in Spanish. . . .

---

*Deep-seated sociopolitical attitudes that cause people to be wary of differences and diversity are at work in school as much as they are in society, and these attitudes must be confronted before real changes can take place.*

---

Perhaps due to the elevated status of English, negative messages about speaking Spanish, students' desires to assimilate, and efforts by the school and parents, developing English proficiency was not a major struggle for most of these students. While 11 of the 13 were considered to have limited proficiency in English at the beginning of fifth grade based on standardized language tests, all had progressed several levels by the end of the year. All but 3 had reached adequate English proficiency by the end of Grade 6, according to school tests. At the beginning of the fifth-grade year, all 13 of the students spoke Spanish when given the choice. Less than 2 years later, only 7 preferred Spanish to English. The remaining 6 were clearly showing a loss of Spanish vocabulary and fluency and were becoming resistant to speaking Spanish. One girl who less than 2 years earlier was extremely timid about English would now *only* speak English, even when interviewed in Spanish because, she said, her Spanish sounded "funny." These patterns of language use—relatively rapid growth in English accompanied by erosion of home language—are consistent with research findings that children of immigrants typically begin to lose their native language by middle school. . . .

Some parents described purposeful strategies for keeping Spanish alive and for dealing with obstacles they encountered. All but two families attended church services in Spanish, and all said they were determined to keep their homes English-free because the children were getting plenty of practice in English at school. As Diana's father said, "*Asi en la escuela pueden hablar puro inglés, y aquí van a hablar el espanol. Así es que así no lo ovidan.*" (So in school they can speak English, and here they're going to speak Spanish. So they won't forget.) Maricela's father agreed that it was up to parents to help children conserve Spanish: "*Bueno eso yo pienso que depende también de lo que uno como padre siempre les está comunicando. Que no se pierda este idioma.*" (I think that it also depends on what the parents are always communicating to them. Not to lose this language.) . . .

## Heritage Language Resistance Is Caused By Many Sources

Some important lessons we learned from this study are that these low-income immigrant parents, most with very little education by U.S. standards, were aware, observant, and involved in their children's education. Despite not knowing English, they devised innovative ways to assess their children's knowledge and fluency and strategies for helping them improve in both languages.

However, in addition to the sociopolitical forces of English hegemony and assimilation, these children were under additional pressures to set aside Spanish in favor of English. First, their families were all recent immigrants and the children might have felt relatively undervalued even within a high-poverty, minority community. Second, the dire economic situations of these families made it necessary for parents to take whatever employment they could get, which sometimes meant one or both parents had to be away from the home for extended periods of time. In some families, this left less time for the active promotion or study of home language and culture. . . .

Loss of a language is only the surface problem. If it were so easy to convince educators that bilingualism in young immigrants is a positive thing, it would have happened years ago. Deep-seated sociopolitical attitudes that cause people to be wary of differences and diversity are at work in schools as much as they are in society, and these attitudes must be confronted before real changes can take place.

In addition to strengthening home–school connections, another positive arena for change is preservice teacher education. Most teachers are middle-class European Americans who have little experience in working with students whose socioeconomic, cultural, and linguistic backgrounds differ from their own. More teacher preparation programs are offering courses on culturally relevant pedagogy with information, experiences, and opportunities for discussion designed to help develop appreciation for diversity and differences. Other promising avenues include providing preservice teachers with carefully structured experiences in the communities and schools in which they will teach, and opportunities to develop personal relationships with students and families. Similar experiences can be provided for in-service teachers. Whether or not one shares the language or culture of the family, teachers can support bilingualism, biliteracy, and positive identification with home language and culture. Schools can help to instill the positive feelings about native languages that are so necessary for developing and maintaining bilingualism by creating conditions in which students' native languages are encouraged and celebrated.

Bilingualism and biliteracy are powerful advantages in academic, linguistic, personal, occupational, and social arenas. While many people have to work hard to learn a second language, the deterioration of a language one already knows is a shameful waste of a child's potential to be, in the eloquent words of [one father] Luis Cavazos, *"vale dos personas"* [worth two persons].

# 7

# Race and Politics Drive the Bilingual Education Controversy

*Owen Eagan*

*Owen Eagan is a public relations and political consultant based in Boston, Massachusetts.*

*When decisions about bilingual education are placed on the ballot, many factors affect voters' choices. Americans want to help children, and their personal experiences, political views and nationality impact their personal convictions about what is best for students. In the end, however, it usually comes down to who spends the most money and makes the most compelling argument, rather than a matter of principle.*

In 1998 Ron Unz, a California millionaire, began what would become a national campaign to end bilingual education. That year, he would place a question on the ballot in California to eliminate bilingual education and replace it with what he billed as a one-year English immersion program.

Bilingual education is the process of providing content-area instruction to Limited English Proficient (LEP) students in their native language while teaching them English. English immersion provides almost exclusive instruction in English with the intent of mainstreaming students after one year.

The ballot question passed in California, 61 percent to 39 percent. It would pass again in Arizona where he sponsored a similar initiative in 2000 that passed 63 percent to 37 percent.

Owen Eagan, "Baseball, Apple Pie and English: Lessons From a Losing Campaign Against an 'English Only' Ballot Measure," *Campaigns & Elections*, vol. 24, October–November 2003, pp. 24–27. Copyright © 2003 Campaigns & Elections, Inc. Reproduced by permission.

In 2002, he brought his campaign to Colorado and Massachusetts. Colorado successfully defeated the initiative with the help of a $3 million contribution from a single donor.

However, the measure passed 68 to 32 percent in Massachusetts, the home of the oldest bilingual education law on the books.

## Political History

Question 2, as it was known in Massachusetts, may have been well meaning in its intent. But in the view of our campaign, the Committee for Fairness to Children and Teachers, together with the Massachusetts Teachers Association and the Massachusetts Federation of Teachers, it had no basis in education research and had been a proven failure.

So what accounted for its overwhelming margin of victory in Massachusetts? The purpose of this article is to provide background for interested parties in their deliberations of this issue going forward and to illustrate the danger of legislating by ballot initiative.

---

*To complicate our task, the opposition's campaign was called "English for the Children," and their tag line was "Teach Kids English." They had framed the debate and distilled it into a sound bite that no one could dispute. Who doesn't want to teach kids English?*

---

Unz said the California ballot initiative, Proposition 227, and his campaign was inspired [in] 1996 when a group of parents protested against bilingual education at the Ninth Street Elementary School in Los Angeles. To indict the system, Unz seized on a figure from the state department of education; since the early 1990s, about 5 percent to 7 percent of LEP students had been "redesignated" as fluent in English each year. He dubbed this the "95 percent annual failure rate."

The no campaign did not have comparative figures with which to directly challenge Unz. Instead, they used researchers' explanations of program effects that were complex and generally boring to journalists. In the end, although the anti-Unz campaign outspent his by nearly 5-to-1, they either never found or failed to utilize a clear, consistent, effective message. Recognizing that he had seized upon a politically popular issue, Unz proceeded to take his campaign to the other states.

Despite the success rate of these initiatives, it is interesting to note that among those most affected, namely Latinos, most voted against them. In California, an exit poll conducted by CNN and the *Los Angeles Times* showed that 63 percent of Latinos voted against the measure. In Massachusetts, an exit poll conducted by the Gaston Institute at the University of Massachusetts at Boston showed 95 percent.

Still, with his victories in hand, Unz has indicated that he might make this a national issue by bringing his proposal to Congress.

## The Political Landscape

Dead and contagious. That's how one of the top political strategists in Massachusetts described our campaign against the ballot measure in the summer of 2002, shortly after I had joined the effort. And that said it all. Dead because we didn't have enough money and weren't considered viable, and contagious because no one wanted to touch our issue.

In October 2001, a ballot question proposing to replace bilingual education with English immersion in Massachusetts was polling with a 77 percent favorable rating. In light of these polling numbers, passage was seen as a forgone conclusion.

It didn't matter that in Massachusetts we were already doing better than California. In each year since the California program had been in place, less than 10 percent of students were redesignated as proficient in English, according to the state department of education. The Boston Public School Department estimated that the transition rate for English learners in Boston was nearly 30 percent per year. Statewide, a government report estimated that 80 percent of students were transitioned after 2.8 years.

To complicate our task, the opposition's campaign was called "English for the Children," and their tag line was "Teach Kids English." They had framed the debate and distilled it into a sound bite that no one could dispute. Who doesn't want to teach kids English?

We wanted to teach kids English, too, but we had to use years of educational research and wonkish arguments to make our case.

We had an arsenal of statistics from some of the foremost education experts in the field. We also hired some of the best consultants in the country. So, armed with our research and our team, we proceeded to test our messages.

---

*Politically, supporting this issue was like saying you supported baseball and apple pie, and the poll numbers reflected this.*

---

## Forming a Strategy

Our polling and focus group research revealed that people were very reluctant to accept either sides' claims of success unless they were heavily credentialed. And even if the failure of the California program could be demonstrated, cost in and of itself was not believable because it was counter-intuitive; how could a program that only lasts a year cost more than a program that lasts several years? Therefore, we needed to explain our cost analyses in detail.

However, there was one provision in the ballot initiative that we thought might have been a silver bullet. The proposal would allow teachers to be sued for using a child's native language to help them learn. The suing of teachers was not believable on two levels. One, participants thought it was so outrageous that they didn't believe it was actually in the initiative, and, two, they didn't believe that teachers would actually be sued. But we discovered we could erode voter support of the initiative well below 50 percent once people saw or heard the actual language of the ballot measure.

Unfortunately, the only way to show this information to every voter we'd need to reach was to include the actual text in TV spots. To reach our targeted voters, we estimated we would need about $3 million worth of paid media.

But fund raising would prove to be difficult, as raising money for a political campaign is much like seeking venture capital for a start-up business. People want to see a business plan and have some assurance that their investment is going to be worthwhile. Even in our own poll, support for the initiative was at 63 percent. It wasn't the 77 percent that was demonstrated earlier, but it was still a sizable margin.

Perhaps worst of all, Mitt Romney, the former Olympics chief and venture capitalist, adopted English immersion as a central plank in his campaign for governor. His support for immersion would be promoted in a constant drumbeat of campaign stump speeches, press events, automated phone calls to voters, and two separate TV spots that we estimated cost more than $1 million.

Politically, supporting this issue was like saying you supported baseball and apple pie, and the poll numbers reflected this.

## Politics by Sound Bite

Over the years, we have seen the ballot initiative process evolve from being a tool giving voters greater freedom from corporate and special interests to a tool used by those same interests to advance their own agendas. Though the most expensive part of any ballot initiative campaign is the use of paid media, there are other hurdles for the ordinary citizen in advancing a cause. For instance, the signature gathering process can be particularly daunting. In Massachusetts, Ron Unz would pay an out-of-state signature-gathering firm roughly $250,000 to collect the nearly 67,000 signatures needed to get his initiative on the ballot.

The campaign with the most money doesn't always win. But it is impossible to win without resources.

Our campaign spent about $650,000. Unz's campaign spent roughly $450,000. Combined with Romney's two television spots, English immersion spent more than $1.45 million total.

To figure out how much money we would need to defeat Question 2, in Massachusetts, we looked to our successful counterparts in Colorado. That campaign spent about $3.1 million. Based on the proportion of registered voters in Massachusetts, we would have needed $4.5 million to achieve the same results.

In addition to the number of voters reached via TV and radio spots, our campaign contacted more than 1 million voter contacts through one form or another. Our staff and volunteers in the field made most of the contacts. The communities in which we were best organized were where we won.

In contrast, Unz had no campaign organization or grassroots support. His in-state support consisted of one paid campaign staff person, who primarily served as his spokesman for the press, and several volunteers.

We had some factors in our favor. Acting Gov. Jane Swift (R) signed a bill allowing school districts to decide which programs to implement, including English immersion. We had the support of all 10 Massachusetts congressmen, both U.S. senators, the majority of daily newspapers and the deans of eight schools of education in the state. However, without enough money for paid media, the voters would barely notice.

But our opponents had an effective message. The simplicity of the message "Teach Kids English" was nearly impossible to overcome. Though we outspent the opposing campaign on paper, Romney's support for the measure outweighed our efforts.

## Attitudes Toward Immigrants

Some wondered if the support of Question 2 was the result of anti-immigrant sentiment. We had wondered the same before embarking upon the research phase. However, what we discovered was that voters generally wanted to do whatever was best for the children.

The only hint of anti-immigrant sentiment we found, if we can fairly call it that, was among some senior voters. For them, bilingual education was almost completely foreign. Massachusetts had only implemented its bilingual education law in 1972, following the passage of the federal Bilingual Education Act of 1968. That came about in response to the alarming failure rates for LEP students as they fell behind in English-only classrooms. Seniors we interviewed thought that since these programs didn't exist for either them, their family or the people they knew, the programs were unnecessary.

*[C]omplex public policy should not be decided by popular vote, but that doesn't mean that questions of this nature should be prevented from making the ballot.*

So was there really no anti-immigrant sentiment? None that registered in polls and focus groups. So the question was, what if it wouldn't register in polls and focus groups? That is, what if this is an issue that people weren't likely to be perfectly honest about? After all, who wants to admit that they're anti-immigrant or to be perceived as anti-immigrant?

It is instructive to look at how this issue played out in a state where an "English only" lost. In Colorado, the "No on

Amendment 31" campaign used similar messaging to the "No on Question 2" campaign in Massachusetts. Their core messages were that the measure would be punitive, that it would be costly because teachers could be sued, and that it took away parental choice regarding their kids' education.

There was also one other message that they stumbled upon by chance. Using a $3 million donation from philanthropist Patricia Stryker (who had a child in a bilingual education program), one of the TV spots the opponents launched was called "Chaos." Its message was that Hispanic children were going to be mainstreamed before they were ready, thereby disrupting their education.

John Britz, a media consultant for the no campaign, said this message came from an interview he did with a suburban, Republican mother, who strongly supported Amendment 31.

When Britz suggested to her that her children might be affected if their teacher's time was occupied dealing more with other children who know little English, she withdrew her support for the initiative.

There have been post-election panel discussions among participants in the Colorado campaign that have suggested other influences that contributed to their win. For example, the Colorado campaign had two years to organize while we only had one.

Would more time have made the difference in Massachusetts? That's questionable. But certainly more time and more money would have.

## The Results Are In

The ballot initiative process isn't perfect, but it provides an important form of checks and balances in our political system. No, complex public policy should not be decided by popular vote, but that doesn't mean that questions of this nature should be prevented from making the ballot.

Many campaigns are won and lost based on their ability to get their message out and, more importantly, how they do it. So what do we do in cases such as ours where a campaign doesn't have enough money to get their message out? The only recourse is to continue to fight for what you believe.

Again, the purpose of this piece is to present a more complete picture on this issue, one beyond the interpretation of the Election Day results on Question 2.

The message for elected officials? Respect the will of the voters but consider all the facts.

The message for the rest of us not immediately impacted by Question 2? The best democracy is ensured by an educated, discerning and active citizenry. For this, we must all do our part.

# 8

# Learning English Encourages Assimilation Into U.S. Workforce

*Linda Chavez*

*Linda Chavez is the Chairman of the Center for Equal Opportunity, based in Washington, D.C. She is also the author of several books.*

*Immigrants are an important part of U.S. history and continue to make this country great. Recent controversy over illegal immigration has created malicious rumors and hard feelings against Mexican immigrants as a whole. Although it is indisputable that immigrants should be documented, it is unfair to skew facts and statistics, or to blame legal immigrants, who are hard-working contributors to society, for the wrongdoing of others from the same country. Most immigrants want to assimilate into American culture, and they should be encouraged to learn English and excel in education so they can make America a stronger nation.*

What to do about immigration—both legal and illegal—has become one of the most controversial public-policy debates in recent memory. But why it has occurred at this particular moment is something of a mystery. The rate of immigration into the U.S., although high, is still below what it was even a few years ago, the peak having been reached in the late 1990's. President Bush first talked about comprehensive immigration reform almost immediately after assuming office, but he put the plan on hold after 9/11 and only reintroduced the idea in 2004. Why the current flap?

By far the biggest factor shaping the popular mood seems to have been the almost daily drumbeat on the issue from political talk-show hosts, most prominently CNN's Lou Dobbs and the Fox News Channel's Bill O'Reilly and Sean Hannity (both of whom also have popular radio shows), syndicated radio hosts Rush Limbaugh, Laura Ingraham, Michael Savage, and G. Gordon Liddy, and a plethora of local hosts reaching tens of millions of listeners each week. Stories about immigration have become a staple of cable news, with sensational footage of illegal crossings featured virtually every day.

Media saturation has led, in turn, to the emergence of immigration as a wedge issue in the still-nascent 2008 presidential campaign. Several aspiring Republican candidates—former House Speaker Newt Gingrich, Senate Majority Leader Bill Frist, and Senator George Allen—have worked to burnish their "get tough" credentials, while, on the other side of the issue, Senator John McCain has come forward as the lead sponsor of a bill to allow most illegal aliens to earn legal status. For their part, potential Democratic candidates have remained largely mum, unsure how the issue plays with their various constituencies.

And then there are the immigrants themselves, who have shown surprising political muscle, especially in response to legislation passed by the House that would turn the illegal aliens among them into felons. Millions of mostly Hispanic protesters have taken to the streets in our big cities in recent months, waving American flags and (more controversially) their own national flags while demanding recognition and better treatment. Though Hispanic leaders and pro-immigrant advocates point to the protests as evidence of a powerful new civil-rights movement, many other Americans see the demonstrators as proof of an alien invasion—and a looming threat to the country's prosperity and unity.

In short, it is hard to recall a time when there has been so much talk about immigration and immigration reform—or when so much of the talk has been misinformed, misleading, and ahistorical. Before policy-makers can decide what to do about immigration, the problem itself needs to be better defined, not just in terms of costs and benefits but in relation to America's deepest values.

---

*Millions of mostly Hispanic protesters have taken to the streets in our big cities in recent months, waving American flags and (more controversially) their own national flags while demanding recognition and better treatment.*

---

## Historical Facts

Contrary to popular myth, immigrants have never been particularly welcome in the United States. Americans have always tended to romanticize the immigrants of their grandparents' generation while casting a skeptical eye on contemporary newcomers. In the first decades of the 20th century, descendants of Northern European immigrants resisted the arrival of Southern and Eastern Europeans, and today the descendants of those once unwanted Italians, Greeks, and Poles are deeply distrustful of current immigrants from Latin America. Congressman Tom Tancredo, a Republican from Colorado and an outspoken advocate of tighter restrictions, is fond of invoking the memory of his Italian immigrant grandfather to argue that he is not anti-immigrant, just anti-illegal immigration. He fails to mention that at the time his grandfather arrived, immigrants simply had to show up on American shores (or walk across the border) to gain legal entry. . . .

The real question is not whether the U.S. has the means to stop illegal immigration—no doubt, with sufficient resources, we could mostly do so—but whether we would be better off as a nation without these workers. Restrictionists claim that large-scale immigration—legal and illegal—has depressed wages, burdened government resources, and acted as a net drain on the economy. The Federation for American Immigration Reform (FAIR), the most prominent of the pressure groups on the issue, argues that, because of this influx, hourly earnings among American males have not increased appreciably in 30 years. As the restrictionists see it, if the U.S. got serious about defending its borders, there would be plenty of Americans willing to do the jobs now performed by workers from abroad. . . .

## A Matter of Perspective

Despite the presence in our workforce of millions of illegal immigrants, the U.S. is currently creating slightly more than two million jobs a year and boasts an unemployment rate of 4.7 percent, which is lower than the average in each of the past four decades. More to the point perhaps, when the National Research Council (NRC) of the National Academy of Sciences evaluated the economic impact of immigration in its landmark 1997 study, "The New Americans: Economic, Demographic, and Fiscal Effects of Immigration," it found only a small negative impact on the earnings of Americans, and even then, only for workers at lower skill and education levels.

> *Providing education and health care to the children of immigrants is particularly expensive, and the federal government picks up only a fraction of the expense.*

Moreover, the participation of immigrants in the labor force has had obvious positive effects. The NRC estimated that roughly 5 percent of household expenditures in the U.S. went to goods and services produced by immigrant labor— labor whose relative cheapness translated into lower prices for everything from chicken to new homes. These price advantages, the study found, were "spread quite uniformly across most types of domestic consumers," with a slightly greater benefit for higher-income households.

Many restrictionists argue that if Americans would simply cut their own lawns, clean their own houses, and care for their own children, there would be no need for immigrant labor. But even if this were true, the overall economy would hardly benefit from having fewer workers. If American women were unable to rely on immigrants to perform some household duties, more of them would be forced to stay home. A smaller labor force would also have devastating consequences when it comes to dealing with the national debt and government-funded entitlements like Social Security and Medicare, a point repeatedly made by former Federal Reserve Board Chairman Alan Greenspan. As he told a Senate committee in 2003, "short of a major increase in immigration, economic growth cannot be safely counted upon to eliminate deficits and the difficult choices that will be required to restore fiscal discipline." The following year, Greenspan noted that offsetting the fiscal effects of our own declining birthrate would require a level of immigration "much larger than almost all current projections assume."

The contributions that immigrants make to the economy must be weighed, of course, against the burdens they impose. FAIR and other restrictionist groups contend that immigrants are a huge drain on society because of the cost of providing public services to them—some $67 to $87 billion a year, according to one commonly cited study. Drawing on numbers from the NRC's 1997 report, FAIR argues that "the net fiscal drain on American taxpayers [from immigration] is between $166 and $226 a year per native household."

There is something to these assertions, though less than may at first appear. Much of the anxiety and resentment generated by immigrants is, indeed, a result of the very real costs they impose on state and local governments, especially in border states like California and Arizona. Providing education and health care to the children of immigrants is particularly expensive, and the federal government picks up only a fraction of the expense. But, again, there are countervailing factors. Illegal immigrants are hardly free-riders. An estimated three-quarters of them paid federal taxes in 2002, amounting to $7 billion in Social Security contributions and $1.5 billion in Medicare taxes, plus withholding for income taxes. They also pay state and local sales taxes and (as homeowners and renters) property taxes. . . .

---

*States that have moved to English-immersion instruction have seen test scores for Hispanic youngsters rise, in some cases substantially.*

---

## The Question of Assimilation

Of equal weight among foes of immigration are the cultural changes wrought by today's newcomers, especially those from Mexico. In his book, Who Are We? The Challenges to National Identity (2004), the eminent political scientist Samuel P. Huntington warns that "Mexican immigration is leading toward the demographic reconquista of areas Americans took from Mexico by force in the 1830's and 1840's." Others have fretted about the aims of militant Mexican-American activists, pointing to "El Plan de Aztlan," a radical Hispanic manifesto hatched in 1969, which calls for "the control of our barrios, campos, pueblos, lands, our economy, our culture, and our political life," including "self-defense against the occupying forces of the oppressors"—that is, the U.S. government.

To be sure, the fantasy of a recaptured homeland exists mostly in the minds of a handful of already well-assimilated Mexican-American college professors and the students they manage to indoctrinate (self-described "victims" who often enjoy preferential admission to college and subsidized or free tuition). But such rhetoric understandably alarms many Americans, especially in light of the huge influx of Hispanic immigrants into the Southwest. Does it not seem likely that today's immigrants—because of their numbers, the constant flow of even more newcomers, and their proximity to their countries of origin—will be unable or unwilling to assimilate as previous ethnic groups have done?

There is no question that some public policies in the U.S. have actively discouraged assimilation. Bilingual education, the dominant method of instruction of Hispanic immigrant children for some 30 years, is the most obvious culprit, with its emphasis on retaining Spanish. But bilingual education is on the wane, having been challenged by statewide initiatives in California (1998), Arizona (2000), and Massachusetts (2004), and by policy shifts in several major cities and at the federal level. States that have moved to English-immersion instruction have seen test scores for Hispanic youngsters rise, in some cases substantially.

---

*It . . . makes sense to require that immigrants have at least a basic knowledge of English and to give preference to those who have advanced skills or needed talents.*

---

Evidence from the culture at large is also encouraging. On most measures of social and economic integration, Hispanic immigrants and their descendants have made steady strides up the ladder. English is the preferred language of virtually all U.S.-born Hispanics; indeed, according to a 2002 national survey by the Pew Hispanic Center and the Kaiser Family Foundation, 78 percent of third-generation Mexican-Americans cannot speak Spanish at all. In education, 86 percent of U.S.-born Hispanics complete high school, compared with 92 percent of non-Hispanic whites, and the drop-out rate among immigrant children who enroll in high school after they come here is no higher than for the native-born.

It remains true that attendance at four-year colleges is lower among Hispanics than for other groups, and Hispanics lag in attaining bachelor's degrees. But neither that nor their slightly lower rate of high-school attendance has kept Hispanic immigrants from pulling their economic weight. After controlling for education, English proficiency, age, and geographic location, Mexican-born males actually earn 2.4 percent more than comparable U.S.-born white males, according to a recent analysis of 2000 Census data by the National Research Council. Hispanic women, for their part, hold their own against U.S.-born white women with similar qualifications. . . .

## Solutions to Real Problems

How, then, to proceed? Congress is under growing pressure to strengthen border control, but unless it also reaches some agreement on more comprehensive reforms, stauncher enforcement is unlikely to have much of an effect. With a growing economy and more jobs than our own population can readily absorb, the U.S. will continue to need immigrants. Illegal immigration already responds reasonably well to market forces. It has increased during boom times like the late 1990's and decreased again when jobs disappear, as in the latest recession. Trying to determine an ideal number makes no more sense than trying to predict how much steel or how many textiles we ought to import; government quotas can never match the efficiency of simple supply and demand. As President Bush has argued—and as the Senate has now agreed—a guest-worker program is the way to go.

Does this mean the U.S. should just open its borders to anyone who wants to come? Hardly. We still need an orderly process, one that includes background checks to insure that terrorists and criminals are not being admitted. It also makes sense to require that immigrants have at least a basic knowledge of English and to give preference to those who have advanced skills or needed talents.

Moreover, immigrants themselves have to take more responsibility for their status. Illegal aliens from Mexico now pay significant sums of money to "coyotes" who sneak them across the border. If they could come legally as guest workers, that same money might be put up as a surety bond to guarantee their return at the end of their employment contract, or perhaps to pay for health insurance. Nor is it good policy to allow immigrants to become welfare recipients or to benefit from affirmative action: restrictions on both sorts of programs have to be written into law and stringently applied. . . .

Regardless of what Congress does or does not do—the odds in favor of an agreement between the Senate and House on final legislation are still no better than 50-50—immigration is likely to continue at high levels for the foreseeable future. Barring a recession or another terrorist attack, the U.S. economy is likely to need some 1.5 to 2 million immigrants a year for some time to come. It would be far better for all concerned if those who wanted to work in the U.S. and had jobs waiting for them here could do so legally, in the light of day and with the full approval of the American people.

## Learning From History to Avoid Repeating It

In 1918, at the height of the last great wave of immigrants and the hysteria that it prompted in some circles, Madison Grant, a Yale-educated eugenicist and leader of the immigration-restriction movement, made a prediction:

> The result of unlimited immigration is showing plainly in the rapid decline in the birth rate of native Americans because the poorer classes of colonial stock, where they still exist, will not bring children into the world to compete in the labor market with the Slovak, the Italian, the Syrian, and the Jew. . . . The man of the old stock is being crowded out of many country districts by these foreigners, just as he is today being literally driven off the streets of New York City

by the swarms of Polish Jews. These immigrants adopt the language of the native American, they wear his clothes, they steal his name, and they are beginning to take his women, but they seldom adopt his religion or understand his ideals, and while he is being elbowed out of his own home, the American looks calmly abroad and urges on others the suicidal ethics which are exterminating his own race.

Today, such alarmism reads as little more than a historical curiosity. Southern and Eastern European immigrants and their children did, in fact, assimilate, and in certain cases—most prominently that of the Jews—they exceeded the educational and economic attainments of Grant's "colonial stock."

Present-day restrictionists point to all sorts of special circumstances that supposedly made such acculturation possible in the past but render it impossible today. Then as now, however, the restrictionists are wrong, not least in their failure to understand the basic dynamic of American nationhood. There is no denying the challenge posed by assimilating today's newcomers, especially so many of them in so short a span of time. Nor is there any denying the cultural forces, mainly stemming from the Left, that have attenuated the sense of national identity among native-born American elites themselves and led to such misguided policies as bilingual education. But, provided that we commit ourselves to the goal, past experience and progress to date suggest the task is anything but impossible.

As jarring as many found the recent pictures of a million illegal aliens marching in our cities, the fact remains that many of the immigrants were carrying the American flag, and waving it proudly. They and their leaders understand what most restrictionists do not and what some Americans have forgotten or choose to deny: that the price of admission to America is, and must be, the willingness to become an American.

# 9

# Latino Parents Don't Want Their Children in Bilingual Education

*Samuel G. Freedman*

*Samuel G. Freedman is a writer for the* New York Times.

*In the controversy surrounding bilingual education, teachers and politicians are usually in the spotlight. However, parents are in the best position to see the effects of English instruction; and, in New York at least, Latino immigrants aren't pleased their children are being forced into bilingual education programs. They say these classes actually hold their children back and keep them from learning English, which will prevent them from having the better life their parents want for them.*

On a sultry night in late June [2004], when the school term was nearly over, two dozen parents gathered in a church basement in Brooklyn to talk about what a waste the year had been. Immigrants from Mexico and the Dominican Republic, raising their children in the battered neighborhood of Bushwick, they were the people bilingual education supposedly serves. Instead, one after the other, they condemned a system that consigned their children to a linguistic ghetto, cut off from the United States of integration and upward mobility.

These parents were not gadflies and chronic complainers. Patient and quiet, the women clad in faded shifts, the men

Samuel G. Freedman, "It's Latino Parents Speaking Out On Bilingual Education Failures," *The New York Times*, July 14, 2004, p. B-9. Copyright © 2004 by The New York Times Company. Reproduced by permission.

shod in oil-stained work boots, they exuded the aura of people reluctant to challenge authority, perhaps because they ascribed wisdom to people with titles, or perhaps because they feared retribution.

With the ballast of one another's company, however, they spoke. Gregorio Ortega spoke about how his son Geraldo, born right here in New York, had been abruptly transferred into a bilingual class at P.S. 123 after spending his first four school years learning in English. Irene De Leon spoke of her daughter being placed in a bilingual section at P.S. 123 despite having done her first year and a half of school in English when the family lived in Queens. Benerita Salsedo wondered aloud why, after four years in the bilingual track at P.S. 145 in Bushwick, her son Alberto still had not moved into English classes. Her two other children were also stuck in bilingual limbo.

"I'm very angry," Ms. Salsedo said in Spanish through an interpreter. "The school is supposed to do what's best for the kids. The school puts my kids' education in danger, because everything is in English here."

*[P]ublic schools shunted Latino children into [bilingual education] even if those pupils had been born in the United States and previously educated in English, and . . . once the child was in the bilingual track it was almost impossible to get out.*

And the children had no trouble expressing their own frustration lucidly enough in English. "I ask the teacher all the time if I can be in English class," said Alberto, a 9-year-old who will enter sixth grade in the fall [of 2004]. "The teacher just says no." For the time being, Alberto added, he learns English by watching the Cartoon Network.

## All Too Familiar

Listening to this litany, I experienced the sensation that Yogi Berra memorably called "déjà vu all over again." Five years earlier, in the rectory of another church only a few blocks away, another group of immigrant parents voiced the identical complaints about bilingual education—that the public schools shunted Latino children into it even if those pupils had been born in the United States and previously educated in English, and that once the child was in the bilingual track it was almost impossible to get out. An association of Bushwick parents, virtually all of them Hispanic immigrants, had gone as far as suing in State Supreme Court in a futile attempt to reform the bilingual program in local schools.

---

*The foes of bilingual education, at least as practiced in New York, are not Eurocentric nativists but Spanish-speaking immigrants who struggled to reach the United States and struggle still at low-wage jobs to stay here so that their children can acquire and rise with an American education, very much including fluency in English.*

---

Back then, the school system's many critics ascribed the bilingual fiasco in Bushwick largely to the failed policy of decentralization. What "community control" meant then in Bushwick was a school district dominated by the neighborhood's City Council member, Victor Robles (now the city clerk). School jobs, including those in bilingual education, were patronage plums.

For years, bilingual education coasted along on its perception as a virtual civil right for Hispanics. Maybe such a reputation was deserved 30 years ago [in the 1970s], when the Puerto Rican Legal Defense Fund sued and won a consent decree requiring that New York City offer bilingual education. But as the innovation hardened into an orthodoxy, and as a sort of employment niche grew for bilingual educators and bureaucrats, the idealistic veneer began to wear away.

The grievances of Bushwick's parents point at an overlooked truth. The foes of bilingual education, at least as practiced in New York, are not Eurocentric nativists but Spanish-speaking immigrants who struggled to reach the United States and struggle still at low-wage jobs to stay here so that their children can acquire and rise with an American education, very much including fluency in English.

## Making Good on Campaign Promises?

As a candidate for mayor, Michael R. Bloomberg assailed the status quo in bilingual education and called for its replacement with English-immersion classes. His pledge rested on firm ground. Reports commissioned by Chancellor Ramon Cortines in 1994 and Mayor Rudolph W. Giuliani in 2000 concluded that children qualified for mainstream classes more rapidly coming from English as a Second Language programs than from bilingual ones. ESL classes take place largely in English; bilingual education in the students' native language.

With decentralization dismantled in 2002 and a hand-picked school chancellor installed the next year, Mayor Bloomberg seemingly backed away. Diana Lam, the top aide to Chancellor Joel I. Klein until her ouster, was both a product and proponent of traditional bilingualism. The mayor now emphasizes improving the existing bilingual program, despite its demonstrable shortcomings.

With Ms. Lam gone, perhaps the mayor and Mr. Klein can fulfill their erstwhile pledges. Carmen Fariña, the new deputy chancellor, yesterday promised large-scale reforms beginning next September. What she means by that is not junking bilingual education or even curtailing its use as much as improving teacher training and incorporating clear performance standards and oversight. Yet the Department of Education already has a highly successful model of ESL instruction in two existing high schools, Bronx International and La Guardia International.

"Bushwick is a test case of how bilingual programs are actually being implemented," said Michael Gecan, a national organizer for the Industrial Areas Foundation, which has worked closely with parents there for more than a decade. "We have great confidence in Klein. We've found him to be very responsive and very aggressive. But we've been concerned about the bilingual effort. This is a large vestige of the old school culture. It remains in the system. And it's intensively guarded by the local politicians and the teachers' union."

In one respect, though, the bilingual program in Bushwick did subscribe to the English-immersion approach. Parent after parent in the church basement remembered receiving, and then naïvely signing, a letter from school that apparently constituted their agreement to having a child put into bilingual classes. The letter, recalled these Spanish-speaking parents, was written only in English.

# 10

# Dual Language Solves Bilingual Education Failures

*Patricia Kilday Hart*

*Patricia Kilday Hart is a writer for* Texas Monthly.

*After years of unsuccessful bilingual education in Texas class-rooms, a new approach is showing promising results. By putting Spanish-speaking students and English speakers in classes together which are taught in only one language, children must help each other, and are fully immersed in two languages. These students become fluent in English and Spanish, score higher on academic testing than those in bilingual classes, and earn scholarships to prestigious universities. Despite this success, state lawmakers are unconvinced dual language programs should be implemented in all Texas schools.*

Two years ago, more than eight out of ten seventh- and eighth-graders with limited English skills failed the Texas Assessment of Knowledge and Skills (TAKS) test. Ninth- and tenth-graders did even worse. These depressing results occurred despite extensive bilingual and English as a second language (ESL) programs and come at a time when the number of students with limited English skill—15.5 percent of the total public school enrollment—has doubled in the past two decades. And yet these students drop out of high school at twice the rate of their counterparts. This is a catastrophe in the making: the noneducation of tomorrow's Texas workforce.

I would like to be able to report that state education officials are on top of this crisis and studying ways to fix it, but it

Patricia Kilday Hart, "Why Juan Can't Read," *Texas Monthly*, vol. 34, October 2006, pp. 104–107. Reprinted with permission from the October 2006 issue of Texas Monthly.

should come as no surprise that this is not the case. In February the Mexican American Legal Defense and Educational Fund (MALDEF) filed a motion contending that the state had failed to live up to agreements it made as a result of a 1981 federal lawsuit that accused Texas of failing to provide Spanish-speaking students equal educational opportunities. In that case, brought before U.S. district judge William Wayne Justice, the state agreed to provide bilingual classes in elementary schools, where academic material would be taught primarily in Spanish, in every school district with at least twenty students in the same grade who had limited English skills. In grades nine through twelve, students who were still identified as having limited English skills were to attend regular classes taught in English and receive special instruction in English as a second language only during a separate class period. Chief among MALDEF's current complaints is that budget cuts have forced the Texas Education Agency [TEA] to all but halt on-site monitoring of bilingual programs to determine whether they are effective. Since 2003, MALDEF argues, the TEA hasn't properly audited those programs, neglecting to determine, for instance, how bilingual ed students (who, after starting with Spanish instruction, are supposed to be increasingly taught in English) are identified as ready to move into classes taught entirely in English. Meanwhile, critics contend that overreliance on Spanish in bilingual programs actually slows the learning of English by Spanish-speaking students. In June the state Republican party adopted a platform plank calling for an end to all bilingual education in public schools.

Why is it that after all these years, Texas schools still have not found an effective way to teach Spanish-speaking students the English language? A major obstacle is a shortage of qualified elementary school bilingual education and ESL teachers, calculated at 2,900 by Texas A&M University researchers in 2002. This shortfall is occurring at the same time that the Spanish-speaking population is exploding. Districts are forced to look for teachers far beyond Texas; Dallas school officials send teams of recruiters to Puerto Rico and Mexico to hire teachers. The lack of teachers has the effect of forcing districts to prematurely push students out of bilingual programs and into English-only classes to make room for newcomers. Critics of bilingual education argue that English-immersion classes—the sooner the better—would be more effective, but the Houston Independent School District recently completed a three-year study whose results suggest the opposite: that bilingual students who are kept in the program until they are ready to graduate into English-only classes actually beat the district's average for all students on standardized tests and performed much better than students who received ESL instruction.

---

*Dual language has helped liberate its students from the grim statistical reality that half of the Hispanic students in Texas will become dropouts. . . .*

---

"The later the better" is also the premise for what I believe is the most promising approach to bilingual education in Texas, an intensive program known as dual language. The idea behind dual language is that non-Spanish-speaking students and non-English-speaking students are put together in the same classroom and taught academic subjects in either all Spanish or all English. The classroom teaching is reinforced by the opportunity for children who speak different languages to rely on one another for help.

Perhaps the best example of a successful dual language program is at Del Valle High School, in the Ysleta Independent School District, in El Paso. Looking for information about dual language online, I came across the YISD's ambitious vision statement, which boldly claims that all of its students will "graduate from high school fluent in two or more languages, prepared and inspired to continue their education in a four-year college, university, or institution of higher education." And so, in May [2006], I visited Del Valle on the giddy day the seniors gathered to practice for graduation. The school's "brag sheet"—listing the college scholarships landed by its graduates—matched up well against those of private schools: a number of students heading for the University of Texas at Austin and others bound for prestigious private colleges like Grinnell, in Iowa. One student had nailed the grand slam of American academic accomplishments: a full-ride scholarship to Harvard University.

This is occurring in a school district that is located on the "wrong" (east) side of El Paso and serves a student population that is 88.1 percent Hispanic and 73.4 percent economically disadvantaged. Dual language has helped liberate its students from the grim statistical reality that half of the Hispanic students in Texas will become dropouts: Ysleta boasts a graduation rate of 84 percent, well above both the Dallas and Houston school districts. A pioneer in dual language, Del Valle in 2005 graduated the first class to begin the program in elementary school. Instead of leaving Spanish behind for all-English classes, students were taught core subjects like algebra and world history in both Spanish and English.

---

*Absorbing two languages takes up brainpower and class time that would ordinarily be spent on other subjects.*

---

Awaiting me in the library was Cindy Sizemore, the coordinator of the dual language program, about two dozen seniors, as well as a few recent graduates. They represented a cross section of interests—football to student council—and, Sizemore confided, a range of academic abilities. Most, she said, came from poor families. The sons and daughters of teachers were considered affluent.

Benito Rodriguez, the student heading to Harvard, told me he had no doubt that the dual language program made the difference in his college application. The son of a self-employed businessman who deals in secondhand tools, Benito said he began losing his fluency in Spanish in first grade when he attended a traditional public school classroom. "I could complain about chores at home, but that was about it," he laughed. After switching to the dual langauge program in fourth grade, he became fully bilingual in English and Spanish and later studied Japanese. Another student, Rudy Garcia, was about to enter UT classified as a sophmore, thanks to the 21 hours of Spanish credits he earned by taking advanced placement classes.

Some of the kids reported hour-long bus rides to get to Del Valle, a magnet school that is one of four high schools in the YISD offering dual language (several elementary and middle schools do as well). Parents and administrators faced another hurdle: In the early years of dual language, students do not score well on standardized tests. Absorbing two languages takes up brainpower and class time that would ordinarily be spent on other subjects. Many parents, fearful that their children are falling behind, pull their students out of dual language in elementary school.

Hortencia Pina, who oversees the dual language program for the Ysleta district, couldn't be more sympathetic: One of her own daughters, a dual language student, stumbled on early grade-school achievement tests. "I can really see where the parents are coming from," she says. "Even if you know the research, you still panic as a parent. You start questioning yourself." (It wasn't until the sixth grade that her daughter passed all the portions of the required tests.) In the beginning it is an adjustment, Pina says, but in time dual language students will surpass kids pushed into a regular classroom too early.

Dual language programs have been blooming across the state, with promising results reported by the Houston, Aldine, Bryan, and San Antonio school districts, to name a few; in all, according to the most recent data available, there are 238 such programs around the state. Rafael Lara-Alecio, a Texas A&M professor of educational psychology who maintains a Web site devoted to the dual language movement (texastwoway.org), says teachers and parents—both Anglo and Hispanic—are beginning to demand them.

The fate of bilingual education, including dual language, will ultimately be determined in the political system. When the Legislature meets again, in January, lawmakers will review formulas that determine how much money school districts get for students who come from impoverished or non-English-speaking backgrounds. For proponents of bilingual education, the debate could hardly come at a worse time. The rancorous opposition to illegal immigration was likely sparked, in part, by voter resentment of escalating school district costs attributable to the children of illegal immigrants. Since Texas already provides extra funding for students with limited English skills, Republican politicians may well balk at giving schools more money for a system that is producing poor results.

El Paso's Democratic state senator, Eliot Shapleigh, wants the dual language immersion pilot program to be expanded into all Texas schools. That's not going to happen, even if he comes armed with an eighteen-year study by professors Wayne P. Thomas and Virginia P. Collier, of George Mason University, in Virginia, titled "The Astounding Effectiveness of Dual Language Education for All." In this political climate, a Republican legislature is not going to mandate that Anglo kids have to enter a bilingual program. Dual language is, and can only be, an elective program that requires parental support, good teachers, and a supply of English-speaking kids, who may not be available in some school districts. At the very least, however, legislators should restore funding to allow the TEA to conduct meaningful oversight of the bilingual programs already in place.

Republican state senator Florence Shapiro, of Plano, the chair of the Senate Education Committee, admits to being "frustrated" by the lack of hard data showing which programs work best in Texas and is "very disappointed" in how little TEA has contributed. "There is no good solid data we can work off of," she laments. But she isn't inclined to throw more money at a program that's not working, as it would only give schools a financial incentive to keep students "wallowing" in bilingual classes they would no longer need if the program were working. David Hinojosa, a MALDEF staff attorney, has a different perspective. He argues that fiscal conservatives want to push students into classes taught in English so the state will no longer have to pay school districts their bilingual stipend. "We think the state should do what it said it was going to do: truly implement a bilingual program," Hinojosa says.

Even if anti-immigration sentiment forestalls bilingual education reform in 2007, it cannot change the reality of Texas's future. The projections of state demographer Steve Murdock, which are widely known around the Capitol, show that the Texas population will be majority Hispanic in twenty to thirty years. If bilingual education continues to fall and Hispanics continue to drop out of school at a rate of 50 percent, what then? Which employers will entrust their bottom line to an uneducated workforce? Who will pay taxes? This is a high-stake issue, and Texas can either get it right—which means dual language—or get it disastrously wrong.

# 11

# "No Child Left Behind" Creates Obstacles for English Language Learners

*Wayne E. Wright*

*Wayne E. Wright is an assistant professor at the University of Texas, San Antonio.*

*When it comes to the No Child Left Behind Act, the federal education policy is leaving behind a large demographic: the Limited English Proficient (LEP) subgroup. According to current mandates, English language learners are required to take state academic assessment exams before they are proficient. These tests create anxiety and fear among English language learners, and cannot accurately gauge the progress these students are making in school. It is time to give these students a genuine opportunity to excel, and to find other ways to measure their learning while they transition into English.*

Early in 2005, I attended a conference for newspaper education reporters in Texas on the effects of No Child Left Behind (NCLB). One of the stars of the event was Sandy Kress, a former education advisor to President George W. Bush and one of the bill's chief architects. Kress gave a powerful and passionate defense of NCLB, describing how, for the first time in history, the federal government was serious about educating all students, how it was finally doing something about closing the achievement gap and improving education for

Wayne E. Wright, "A Catch-22 For Language Learners," *Educational Leadership*, vol. 64, no. 3, November 2006, pp. 22–27. Copyright © 2006 by the Association for Supervision and Curriculum Development. All rights reserved. Used by permission.

poor and minority students. With the air of the attorney he is, he rejected the criticisms of NCLB made by the speakers who preceded him. However, when asked about English language learners, he chuckled and then admitted that no one really knew what to do with them. All he knew, he said, was that they needed to be included somehow in testing and accountability programs.

This lack of clarity regarding English language learners (ELLs) is most obvious in the way that NCLB handles the Limited English Proficient (LEP) subgroup. As with other subgroups, such as African Americans or Latinos, the LEP subgroup is expected to make adequate yearly progress (AYP) toward proficiency. By 2014, all English language learners, regardless of how long they have been in the United States, must pass their state's accountability tests. Moreover, if the requisite number of English language learners in a school's LEP subgroup does not pass the tests in a given year, the school is deemed as failing and may be subjected to sanctions.

When it comes to English language learners, NCLB defies logic. Common sense dictates that if you administer a test to students in a language they don't understand, they probably won't do well on it. NCLB contradicts itself on this very point. The law describes a limited English proficient student as one "whose difficulties in speaking, reading, writing, or understanding the English language may be sufficient to deny the individual the ability to meet the State's proficient level of achievement on State assessments". Nevertheless, NCLB mandates that English language learners do just that, and schools are punished if they don't.

The biggest flaw, however, is the way AYP is calculated for the LEP subgroup. The LEP subgroup is treated the same as other subgroups, such as those based on ethnicity/race. But unlike students in the ethnicity/race subgroups, who obviously remain in the same category, students continually move in and out of the LEP subgroup. Even more problematic, those students who speak the most English—and thus who are more likely to pass the test—leave the LEP subgroup only to be replaced by newly arrived English language learners who speak the least English. This makes it impossible for the LEP subgroup to show consistent growth.

In partial acknowledgement of these flaws, then U.S. Secretary of Education Rod Paige announced in February 2004 two modifications that states could take advantage of: They could exclude LEP students from the reading/language arts test during their first year in the United States, and they could include English language learners who had attained English proficiency in the LEP subgroup for up to two years.

---

*Even when students had a dictionary, few actually used them. Many didn't know how; others were embarrassed to use them in front of their peers.*

---

These changes are insufficient, however. First, few English language learners can learn enough English in one year to pass their state's reading test. Second, the students must still take their state's math test their first year in the United States, even if they arrive on the day of the test. And contrary to what some might think, math tests do not pose less of a challenge to English language learners than English tests do. These tests include a great deal of language, which might explain why English language learners in Arizona scored lower in their state's math assessment than they did in reading and writing. As for keeping former English language learners in the LEP subgroup for two additional years, this strategy only delays the problem rather than solves it.

## "Reasonable Accommodations"

NCLB requires schools to test English language learners in a "valid and reliable manner." Schools are to provide "reasonable accommodations," including, "to the extent practicable," administering tests in students' native languages until the students attain proficiency in English. Although these requirements sound reasonable, they actually introduce several problems. First, the law neither defines "accommodations" nor defines what constitutes "reasonable." Second, no monitoring mechanisms are in place to ensure that schools actually provide accommodations. Third, there is no consensus on what constitutes an acceptable accommodation; thus state accommodation policies vary substantially. Finally, little research has been conducted on the most effective accommodations for English language learners, and the research that does exist on how schools can provide accommodations while maintaining test validity and reliability is inconclusive. In short, NCLB requires something that we don't yet know how to do.

A survey that I conducted of teachers in 40 Arizona elementary schools with substantial English language learner populations revealed that fewer than half of these schools provided accommodations on the state test. Because teachers received conflicting information about accommodations, practices varied widely. Some teachers were allowed to read the directions or questions aloud in English; others were allowed to translate them. Some teachers permitted students to use English or bilingual dictionaries. Most teachers reported that these accommodations were of little benefit, however. One teacher noted that her school had only five Spanish-English dictionaries to share across 27 classrooms. Even when students had a dictionary, few actually used them. Many didn't know how; others were embarrassed to use them in front of their peers. Even in those instances in which translation was permitted, few students requested it.

Teachers from the Arizona survey described the behaviors of their English language learners as the students took the state test: Seventy-eight percent reported instances of students complaining that they could not understand the test questions, 68 percent reported instances of students leaving entire sections of the test blank, and 78 percent reported instances of students randomly bubbling in answers without reading the questions. Although these teachers believed that schools should be held accountable for their effectiveness in teaching English language learners, 78 percent thought that high-stakes tests were not appropriate for this purpose, and 90 percent thought that these tests did not provide an accurate measure of English language learners' academic achievement.

Teachers also worried about the effect of these tests on students. During testing, 88 percent of teachers surveyed had observed English language learners becoming visibly upset, 71 percent had seen students cry, 68 percent had seen students get physically ill, and 35 percent had seen students throw up.

---

*Given the myriad of problems associated with testing English language learners in English, testing students in their native language appears to be the best accommodation.*

---

## Testing Math in Texas

Texas has extensive "linguistically accommodated testing" (LAT) guidelines for its state math test. For a study of a Texas intermediate school, I served as a volunteer mentor/tutor for two newcomer 5th grade students from Cambodia—Nitha and Bora (Wright & Li, in press). Neither spoke English when they arrived two months into the school year. Nevertheless, they were required to take—and expected to pass—the state math test in English. Despite the extensive LAT guidelines, Nitha and Bora took the same math test as their English-fluent peers, and with no accommodations. Bora got seven of the 44 questions correct; Nitha, who was more skilled in math, only got six correct. Their teacher reported (with a laugh) that during the test, Bora bubbled in five answers in a row and then enthusiastically yelled out "Bingo!" How's that for testing English language learners in a "valid and reliable manner"?

Before the test, I provided Nitha and Bora with weekly math tutoring sessions in Khmer (Cambodian). The school hoped that I could provide translation assistance on the day of the test. However, the state denied this request because I was not a district employee. Then the school hoped that I could provide a glossary of math terms in English with Khmer translations. The state also denied this request because the classroom teacher could not verify that the glossary only contained word-for-word translations rather than explanations.

LAT procedures indicated that Nitha and Bora could ask their teacher to read test questions aloud. Even though the students understood that they could request this, they never did. Despite their progress learning English in the six months that they had been in the United States, they simply didn't understand enough of the language to comprehend math questions read aloud.

Even if they had been English-proficient, they still lacked sufficient math knowledge to answer the questions. Nitha and Bora came from an impoverished village in Cambodia. Their school lacked running water and electricity, and their teachers had less than a high school education. There were not enough textbooks for the students, and the math curriculum was substantially below U.S. standards. Despite being good students in Cambodia, Nitha and Bora were far behind their U.S. peers.

## The Problems with Native-Language Tests

Given the myriad of problems associated with testing English language learners in English, testing students in their native language appears to be the best accommodation. However, native-language tests are only required "to the extent practicable"—and few states have found them practicable. Translating a state test into another language doesn't automatically produce a valid and reliable instrument covering the same concepts at the same level of difficulty. Creating valid and reliable native-language tests requires following the same procedures that produce a valid and reliable English language test. This is an expensive and time-consuming process that few states can afford to undertake. Although the majority of English language learners in the United States are Spanish speakers, the remaining English language learners represent more than 400 different language groups. The numbers of Spanish-speaking English language learners may be high enough to justify creating tests in Spanish—that approach would certainly make sense for students in Spanish/English bilingual programs—but how many states would find it practicable to develop tests in Chinese, Hmong, Arabic, Urdu, and Af Maay?

In addition, non-English tests only work when English language learners can read, write, and receive content instruction through their native language. Developing tests in Khmer, Lao, or Vietnamese is not feasible because few Southeast Asian American students can read or write in their native languages. Even for students like Nitha and Bora, who can read Khmer well, a Khmer version of the math test would have been of little help because nearly all their math instruction has been in English since their arrival in the United States.

---

*Federal education policy is out of touch with the United States' need for bilingual citizens.*

---

## Manipulating the Numbers

Given these technical flaws and the empty promise of accommodations, many states now understand the best strategy for LEP subgroup success: It's not having an LEP subgroup. Some states are setting a high cutoff for the number of students that a school must count as a subgroup. For example, in Arizona, schools need at least 30 English language learners at the same tested grade level to have an LEP subgroup. In 2004, this minimum group size rule enabled 680 Arizona schools to avoid a failing designation. Other states, such as Texas, have set their minimum group size at 50 students or more. This has helped many Texas schools avoid having an LEP subgroup, and not a single school in the state has had an Asian or Native American subgroup.

Each state can determine its minimum subgroup size, and thus far the federal government has made no effort to standardize how states determine that number. NCLB is vague on this point. The only schools that end up having LEP subgroups are those with substantial English language learner populations, and these schools are generally overcrowded, underfunded, and have the least experienced teachers.

Until recently, states were also able to negotiate separate deals with the U.S. Department of Education. For example, during the past few years, Arizona had approval to exclude from AYP calculations the test scores of English language learners who were enrolled for fewer than four years. This strategy alone excluded many English language learners, particularly those who were least likely to pass the tests.

In July 2006, however, the Department of Education informed Arizona—and other states that had these exclusions in effect, such as New York, that it will no longer allow these exclusions. As a result, more than 122 additional schools in Arizona will be labeled as failing to make AYP. Arizona's superintendent of schools has filed a lawsuit against the federal government in an attempt to maintain these exclusions of English language learner test scores.

Apparently, few teachers and school administrators realize that exclusions of their English language learners' test scores are taking place. In the Arizona study, 98 percent of the teachers reported being under pressure to raise English language learners' test scores. In addition, 93 percent of the teachers said that preparing students for high-stakes tests was preventing them from focusing on the students' linguistic and cultural needs. Few of their schools required English as a second language (ESL) instruction, and most did not even have ESL curricular materials. Rather than teach ESL, teachers were required to provide a test-preparation–based curriculum. Even when teachers were able to raise the scores of their English language learners, they did not equate this with effective teaching.

---

*Most of the problems of testing English language learners go away if we simply have patience and give students the opportunity and support to first learn English and then learn academic content.*

---

## Only English Spoken Here

An additional problem with NCLB is its exclusive focus on English. Although bilingual education is still permitted (if state governments allow it), the term "bilingual" has been stripped from federal education law along with any recognition of the individual and societal benefits of bilingualism. Even after-school heritage-language programs are being affected because low-scoring English language learners are often required to attend after-school test-preparation programs instead.

Federal education policy is out of touch with the United States' need for bilingual citizens. It's also out of touch with the priorities and goals of other federal agencies. Foreign language experts testified at the National Briefing on Language and National Security in 2002 that "the U.S. government's language capabilities remain grossly inadequate" and that "we need more linguists in more languages at higher levels of proficiency than ever before." A job recruiter from the U.S. State Department expressed her frustration with finding heritage language speakers with sufficient proficiency in their native languages to qualify as translators. She lamented, "The attempt made in our private and public schools to annihilate any knowledge of the language spoken at home has been very successful" (National Foreign Language Center and National

Security Education Program, 2002). Very successful indeed. In this crucial area of need, NCLB is a giant leap backward.

## It's Just Common Sense

Teachers are not opposed to accountability, but most agree that English language learners should be excluded from the regular state tests, at least until they are proficient enough in English to meaningfully participate. Moreover, given NCLB's internal contradictions—such as requiring students who don't speak English to pass tests in English and setting expectations that are mathematically impossible to attain—it's no wonder the U.S. Department of Education allows states to use a variety of strategies to ensure that the fewest number of schools end up with LEP subgroups. Because so many states are already excluding the scores of so many English language learners from their AYP calculations, why make students take the test at all?

Most of the problems of testing English language learners go away if we simply have patience and give students the opportunity and support to first learn English and then learn academic content. Let's encourage schools to adopt high-quality language programs that ensure that English language learners become the well-educated bilingual citizens that the United States so desperately needs. And let's remove the burden of preparing English language learners for state tests from teachers so they can focus instead on their students' linguistic, cultural, and academic needs.

Native-language tests are only required "to the extent practicable" and few states have found them practicable.

# 12

# Quality of Education Matters More Than Language

*Kendra Hamilton*

*Kendra Hamilton is a writer and the assistant editor of* Black Issues in Higher Education.

*When it comes to teaching English, research shows there is no one right way. Bilingual education and English-only programs can both be successful. What really matters is the quality of the instruction given. Unfortunately, in a controversy charged by media hype and political strategies, few advocates on either side pause to consider that no education is one-size-fits-all, that children do not all learn the same way, and that the real issue is not which program is better, but what is best for the students.*

Eight years ago, Proposition 227 virtually eliminated bilingual education in California's K–12 schools. Since then, the English-only approach has made inroads in states like Arizona and Massachusetts, where ballot initiatives have created even more restrictive "English immersion" programs than California's. In Colorado, backers of a failed ballot initiative are trying again, this time with a campaign for a constitutional amendment.

But a group of new studies is providing fresh evidence of what many researchers have been saying all along: English immersion has more political appeal than educational merit.

Kendra Hamilton, "Bilingual or Immersion? A New Group of Studies Is Providing Fresh Evidence That It's Not the Language of Instruction That Counts, But the Quality of Education," *Diverse Issues in Higher Education*, vol. 23, April 20, 2006, p. 23. Copyright 2006 © Diverse: Issues in Higher Education, a CMA publication. Cox, Matthews, and Associates. Reproduced by permission.

"We're saying it's not possible given the data available to definitively answer the question 'which is better—bilingual or immersion?'" says Dr. Amy Merickel, co-author of "Effects of the Implementation of Proposition 227 on the Education of English Learners K–12." The five-year, $2.5 million study was conducted for the state of California by the American Institutes for Research and WestEd.

"We don't see conclusive evidence that bilingual education is superior to English immersion, and we don't see conclusive evidence for the reverse," Merickel says. "We think it's the wrong question. It's not the model of instruction that matters—it's the quality."

Dr. Tim Shanahan, professor of curriculum and instruction at the University of Illinois-Chicago and director of its Center for Literacy, agrees.

Shanahan and a team of more than a dozen researchers from institutions across the nation recently completed a synthesis of all the available research on literacy, including second language literacy, for the U.S. Department of Education.

"When we looked at all the past attempts to get at this issue and analyzed their data, essentially what we concluded was that, in fact, kids did somewhat better if they received some amount of instruction in their home language," Shanahan says. "How much? It was not clear from the available data. What should it look like? That wasn't entirely clear either. But across the board, the impact of some instruction in home language seemed to be beneficial.

"But one of the things that surprised me and that stood out for me was the sheer volume of the research that was not devoted to these issues," he adds. "If you look at the data, most of the research is on [which] language of instruction [is better]. That issue has so sucked up all the oxygen that all those other issues of quality clearly are being neglected."

## Results Don't Validate
## English-Only Advocates' Claims

Such conclusions run sharply counter to the assertions of many defenders of English immersion. In 1997, millionaire Ron Unz began a campaign against bilingual education, forming an advocacy organization with a simple name and message—English for the Children. That organization helped push Proposition 227 to a landslide victory in California, claiming 61 percent of the vote. Two years later, citing dramatic gains on test scores for immigrant children, the English for the Children movement moved to Arizona, where Proposition 203 notched 63 percent of the vote. In 2002, Massachusetts followed suit with Question 2, which was passed with 70 percent support. But in Colorado, voters rejected the English-immersion philosophy, turning it down 55 percent to 44 percent at the polls.

But the movement began to fizzle after 2002. The offices of English for the Children have closed, and studies have consistently been punching holes in core tenets of the English-only argument.

First to fall were the "dramatic gains" in test scores. Proponents of English-immersion stated emphatically that test scores for immigrant students had shot up 40 percent between 1998 and 2000. But research teams from Stanford University, Arizona State University and others pointed out that scores had risen for all students during that period. They also noted that the rising test scores were due to the fact that California had introduced a new achievement test and not to the effects of Prop 227.

More damning was the failure of Prop 227 to hold up its central promise. English for the Children had repeatedly claimed that results could be achieved with only a one-year transition period for English learners.

"The one-year limit is a fantasy," says Dr. Stephen Krashen, professor emeritus at the University of Southern California's

Rossier School of Education. "In California and Arizona, English learners are currently gaining less than one level per year out of five, where level five means 'ready for the mainstream.'

"That means that a child starting with no English will take at least five years before 'transitioning.' In Massachusetts, after three years of study, only half of the English learners are eligible to be considered for regular instruction," he says.

---

*The dropout rate is 31 percent for language minority children who speak English, compared with 51 percent for language minority kids who do not and only 10 percent for the general population.*

---

Merickel's AIR/WestEd research team noted several exemplary programs during the course of their study. Some of the programs were bilingual, others were English immersion and some were "dual immersion"—providing instruction in both Spanish and English.

Prop 227 has actually been a useful tool, she says, for forcing the state to focus much-needed attention on the non-English speaking population. Some former foes of the proposition, she says, "have come to see it as a positive thing."

## A Harsh Downside

But Shelly Spiegel-Coleman, president of Californians Together, an advocacy coalition formed in 1998, isn't willing to go so far.

"The truth is Prop 227 was a horrible blow for us, but if that was all that happened to us since 1998, we could have galvanized attention, made our points" and worked to ease the law's most restrictive elements, she says.

But Prop 227 was the first of a wave of reform movements, each more restrictive than its predecessor. First came a flurry of one-size-fits-all, skill-based reading programs, crafted to meet the curricular needs specified in Prop. 227.

"They allow no accommodation for non-native speakers, and they're sweeping the country." Spiegel-Coleman says.

And then there are the harsh accountability systems mandated by No Child Left Behind.

"There are these people who have so much invested in these English-only reading programs and accountability systems who do not want to admit that what they're doing is wrong for kids," Spiegel-Coleman says.

Indeed, the stakes in these political battles over education could not be higher. According to U.S. Census figures, the number of children living in homes where English is not the primary language more than doubled from 1979 to 1999, from 6 million to 14 million. California was home to more than 1.4 million English learners—nearly 40 percent of all such public school students in the nation (excluding Puerto Rico).

These "language minority" students face formidable obstacles in school, according to the National Center for Education Statistics. The dropout rate is 31 percent for language minority children who speak English, compared with 51 percent for language minority kids who do not and only 10 percent for the general population.

## Changing Status Quo

"At some point," says Shanahan, "we better get serious about immigration, about integrating immigrants as productive, tax-paying and Social Security-supporting parts of our work force. To do these things, they have to be able to do the work that we do in the United States—that means we have to be making quality choices to provide them with a quality education."

But the discussion about quality has only begun, says Shanahan, noting that his review found only 17 studies concerned with educational quality, compared with more than 450 studies examining types of reading programs.

Meanwhile the discussion about the language of instruction—discussion Shanahan says is deeply political—seems never-ending.

# Organizations to Contact

*The editors have compiled the following list of organizations concerned with the issues debated in this book. The descriptions are derived from materials provided by the organizations. All have publications or information available for interested readers. The list was compiled on the date of publication of the present volume; the information provided here may change. Be aware that many organizations take several weeks or longer to respond to inquiries, so allow as much time as possible.*

**California Association for Bilingual Education**
16033 E. San Bernardino Road, Covina, CA   91722-3900
(626) 814-4441 • fax: (626) 814-4640
e-mail: info@bilingualeducation.org
Web site: www.bilingualeducation.org

The California Association for Bilingual Education (CABE) promotes quality bilingual education for students in California. CABE honors the rich multicultural and global society, recognizing that respecting diversity makes for a stronger state and nation.

**Center for Equal Opportunity**
7700 Leesburg Pike, Suite 231, Falls Church, VA   22043
(703) 442-0066 • fax: (703) 442-0449
Web site: www.ceousa.org

The Center for Equal Opportunity (CEO) is devoted to promoting colorblind equal opportunity and racial harmony in the areas of racial preference, immigration and assimilation, and multicultural education.

**CentroNía**
1420 Columbia Rd. NW, Washington, DC   20009
(202) 332-4200 • fax: (202) 745-2562

e-mail: info@centronia.org
Web site: www.centronia.org

CentroNía provides quality education, professional development, and family-support services to low-income multiethnic families. It also manages the DC Bilingual Public Charter School in Washington, DC.

**English First**
8001 Forbes Place, Suite 102, Springfield, VA   22151
(703) 321-8818 • fax: (703) 321-7636
e-mail: info@englishfirst.org
Web site: www.englishfirst.org

English First provides resources and updates on U.S. government legislation regarding bilingual education.

**English for the Children**
555 Bryant St., #371, Palo Alto, CA   94301
(650) 853-0360 • fax: (650) 853-0362
e-mail: info@English4Children.org
Web site: www.onenation.org

English for the Children aims to teach English to all America's children and end bilingual education nationwide.

**Intercultural Development Research Association**
5835 Callaghan Rd., Suite 350, San Antonio, TX   78228-1190
(210) 444-1710 • fax: (210) 444-1714
e-mail: contact@idra.org
Web site: www.idra.org

The Intercultural Development Research Association (IDRA) targets minority, economically disadvantaged, limited English proficient, and gifted and talented students and seeks to promote equal education opportunities for success for these students through the development of curricula based on extensive research.

## National Association for Bilingual Education

1313 L Street NW, Suite 210, Washington, DC   20005

(202) 898-1829 • fax: (202) 789-2866

e-mail: nabe@nabe.org

Web site: www.nabe.org

The National Association for Bilingual Education (NABE) supports the education of English language learners through partnerships with other civil rights and education organizations, grassroots advocacy mobilizing parents, communities for educational equity, and political campaigns to educate the public on bilingual education.

## National Association for Multicultural Education

5272 River Rd., Suite 430, Bethesda, MD   20816

(301) 951-0022 • fax: (301) 951-0023

e-mail: name@nameorg.org

Web site: www.nameorg.org

The National Association for Multicultural Education (NAME) works to bring together individuals and groups from all levels of education, academic disciplines, and diverse educational institutions and careers who share a common interest in multicultural education.

## ProEnglish

1601 N. Kent St., Suite 1100, Arlington, VA   22209

(703) 816-8821 • fax: (571) 527-2813

e-mail: email@proenglish.org

Web site: www.proenglish.org

ProEnglish seeks to enact legislation identifying English as the official language of the United States by appealing to the courts as well as to public opinion.

## Teachers of English to Speakers of Other Languages

700 S. Washington St., Suite 200, Alexandria, VA   22314

(888) 547-3369 • fax: (703) 836-6447

e-mail: info@tesol.org
Web site: www.tesol.org

Teachers of English to Speakers of Other Languages (TESOL) aims to strengthen effective instruction and learning of English while respecting individual rights. The organization provides information to students, schools, and professionals involved in English as a second (or foreign) language around the world, and promotes research and teacher certification.

**Texas Association for Bilingual Education**
5835 Callaghan Rd., #301, San Antonio, TX   78228
(800) 822-3930 • fax: (210) 979-6485
e-mail: tabe@sbcglobal.net
Web site: www.tabe.org

Texas Association for Bilingual Education (TABE) pursues the implementation of effective bilingual-bicultural programs which promote academic excellence for language minority students and equal educational opportunity.

**U.S. English, Inc.**
1747 Pennsylvania Ave. NW, Suite 1050
Washington, DC   20006
(202) 833-0100 • fax: (202) 833-0108
e-mail: info@usaenglish.org
Web site: www.us-english.org/inc

U.S. English, Inc. is the largest citizens' action group dedicated to preserving English as the unifying language of the United States. The organization believes that establishing English as the official language will expand opportunities for immigrants to succeed in the United States.

# Bibliography

## Books

| | |
|---|---|
| Carlos Kevin Blanton | *The Strange Career of Bilingual Education in Texas, 1836–1981*. College Station: Texas A&M University Press, 2004. |
| Maria Estela Brisk | *Bilingual Education: From Compensatory to Quality Schooling*, 2nd ed. Mahwah, NJ: Lawrence Erlbaum Associates, 2006. |
| Stephen J. Caldas | *Raising Bilingual-Biliterate Children in Monolingual Cultures*. Buffalo, NY: Multilingual Matters Limited, 2006. |
| Angela Creese and Peter Martin, eds. | *Multilingual Classroom Ecologies: Inter-Relationships, Interactions, and Ideologies*. Buffalo, NY: Multilingual Matters Limited, 2003. |
| Beth Harry and Janette Klingner | *Why Are So Many Minority Students in Special Education?: Understanding Race & Disability in Schools*. New York: Teachers College Press, 2005. |
| Victoria-Maria MacDonald, ed. | *Latino Education in the United States: A Narrated History from 1513–2000*. New York: Palgrave-Macmillan, 2004. |

| Guadalupe San Miguel Jr. | *Contested Policy: The Rise and Fall of Federal Bilingual Education in the United States, 1960–2001.* Denton, TX: University of North Texas Press, 2004. |
| --- | --- |
| Sonia Nieto | *Language, Culture, and Teaching: Critical Perspectives for a New Century.* Mahwah, NJ: Lawrence Erlbaum Associates, 2002. |
| Terry A. Osborn, ed. | *Language and Cultural Diversity in U.S. Schools: Democratic Principles in Action.* Lanham, MD: Rowman & Littlefield Education, 2007. |
| Aneta Pavlenko, ed. | *Bilingual Minds: Emotional Experience, Expression, and Representation.* Buffalo, NY: Multilingual Matters Limited, 2006. |
| Bertha Perez | *Becoming Biliterate: A Study of Two-Way Bilingual Immersion Education.* Mahwah, NJ: Lawrence Erlbaum Associates, 2004. |
| Kim Potowski | *Language and Identity in a Dual Immersion School.* Buffalo, NY: Multilingual Matters Limited, 2007. |

## Periodicals

| Jamal Abedi, Carolyn Huie Hofstetter, and Carol Lord | "Assessment Accommodations for English Language Learners: Implications for Policy-Based Empirical Research," *Review of Educational Research*, Spring 2004. |
| --- | --- |

Caley S. Americam — "This Is America; We Speak English and Nothing Is For Free," *People's Voice*, May 2006.

Amy Azzam — "A Look at Language Learning," *Educational Leadership*, December 2004–January 2005.

James Banks — "Teaching for Social Justice, Diversity, and Citizenship in a Global World," *Educational Forum*, Summer 2004.

Jim Boulet, Jr. — "Assimilation, Not Amnesty," *National Review*, August 2001.

Andrew Sangpil Byon — "Language Socialization in Korean-as-a-Foreign-Language Classrooms," *Bilingual Research Journal*, Summer 2006.

Alan Cheung and Robert E. Slavin — "How Do English Language Learners Learn to Read?" *Educational Leadership*, March 2004.

Cathy Coulter and Mary Lee Smith — "English Language Learners in a Comprehensive High School," *Bilingual Research Journal*, Summer 2006.

Eugene E. Garcia and Bryant Jensen — "Helping Young Hispanic Learners," *Educational Leadership*, March 2007.

Rick Green — "Bilingual Program Falling Short," *Hartford Courant*, June 19, 2001.

Stephen Krashen — "Skyrocketing Scores: An Urban Legend," *Educational Leadership*, December 2004/January 2005.

| | |
|---|---|
| Jin Sook Lee and Eva Oxelson | "'It's Not My Job': K–12 Teacher Attitudes Toward Students' Heritage Language Maintenance," *Bilingual Research Journal*, Summer 2006. |
| Sarah J. McCarthey, et al. | "Understanding Writing Contexts for English Language Learners," *Research in the Teaching of English*, 2004. |
| Loreta Medina, ed. | "Bilingual Education," *School Library Journal*, April 2005. |
| Kate Menken | "Teaching to the Test: How No Child Left Behind Impacts Language Policy, Curriculum, and Instruction for English Language Learners," *Bilingual Research Journal*, Summer 2006. |
| Luis C. Moll and Elizabeth Arnot-Hopffer | "Sociocultural Competence in Teacher Education," *Journal of Teacher Education*, March 2005. |
| Jay Nordlinger | "Bassackwards: Construction Spanish and Other Signs of the Times," *National Review*, January 29, 2007. |
| Jean Phinney, Irma Romero, Monica Nava, and Dan Huang | "The Role of Language, Parents, and Peers in Ethnic Identity Among Adolescents in Immigrant Families," *Journal of Youth and Adolescence*, April 2001. |
| Peter Schrag | "What's Good Enough? Advocates Are Demanding Not Just Equal but Decent Schools for All Children," *Nation*, May 3, 2004. |
| Diane Smith | "A One-*Dos* Punch," *Fort Worth Star-Telegram*, April 10, 2007. |

| | |
|---|---|
| Guillermo Solano-Flores and Elise Trumball | "Examining Language in Context: The Need for New Research Paradigms in the Testing of English Language Learners," *Educational Researcher*, March 2003. |
| Greg Toppo | "Is Bilingual Education Report Being Downplayed?" *USA Today*, August 25, 2005. |
| Ana María Villegas and Tamara Lucas | "Preparing Culturally Responsive Teachers," *Journal of Teacher Education*, January 1, 2002. |

# Index